Take 5! for Science

150 prompts that build writing and critical-thinking skills

KAYE HAGLER AND JUDY ELGIN JENSEN

Take 5! for Science: 150 prompts that build writing and critical-thinking skills

By Kaye Hagler and Judy Elgin Jensen

Cover Design: Charmaine Whitman
Book Design: Rick Korab

Photo Credits: All photos from Terry Hagler

Library of Congress Cataloging-in-Publication Data

Cataloging-in-publication information is on file with the Library of Congress.

978-1-4966-0292-3 (pbk.)
978-1-4966-0293-0 (eBook PDF)
978-1-4966-0294-7 (eBook)

Maupin House publishes professional resources for K–12 educators. Contact us for tailored, in-school training or to schedule an author for a workshop or conference. Visit www.maupinhouse.com for free lesson plan downloads.

Maupin House Publishing, Inc. by Capstone Professional
1710 Roe Crest Drive
North Mankato, MN 56003
www.maupinhouse.com
888-262-6135
info@maupinhouse.com

Many of the additional resources in this book suggest search terms for the Internet, while others show specific links. These links were operational at the time this book went to press.

Acknowledgments

For all their assistance, patience, and cooperation, we are grateful to our husbands Terry Hagler and Timothy Jensen. The late night hours and takeout food made it possible for this work to be completed. Timothy's physics background also ensured that this biology teacher's physical science was on track. A warm thank you to him. Also a special thank you to Ashley Weeks for her invaluable assistance.

For all teachers who diligently work to engage their students in science and writing, we hope this proves to be a worthwhile tool for your classrooms.

We especially acknowledge the work of Karen Soll at Capstone Professional and Lynnette Brent Maddox for their attention to detail and words of encouragement. We'd also like to acknowledge Terry Hagler, who provided the photographs for this book.

Table of Contents

Introduction

Take 5! for Science
takes students on
a yearlong journey
through the three
main branches of
science—Earth, Life,
and Physical.

It's Time to *Take 5! for Science*

From orbiting the sun to exploring the South Pole, students will go on a journey as they jump into each prompt in *Take 5! for Science*. Each book in the *Take 5!* series focuses on specific learning skills as students design, organize, create, and debate their way through an entire year of prompts, responding to real or imagined situations. Unlike the first book in the *Take 5!* series, *Take 5! for Language Arts*, this time we dig . . . science.

Take 5! for Science takes students on a yearlong journey through the three main branches of science—Earth, Life, and Physical—with two writing prompts for each topic: an **Explore** prompt, suitable for emerging learners, and a **Dig Deeper** prompt for those more fluent in writing skills. The latest Next Generation Science Standards, adopted in 2013, guide the science involved in the prompts. Explore prompts are aligned with the K–2 standards and Dig Deeper prompts are aligned with the 3–5 standards.

Each *Take 5!* prompt helps to set the pace for those first five to 10 minutes of instruction. No one sits waiting for the "official" beginning of class. The class has already begun.

While most prompts are for individual learners, others might be worked on in pairs or in collaboration with other students. You may use whatever strategies work best in grouping students. Like high school lab partners, student pairs put their heads together to create a combined response. Those prompts, labeled "collaboration," will call for a team effort as students explore the many possibilities of each challenge.

The Science Information provided on the teacher page serves as a mini refresher for you on each topic. Filled with pertinent facts and conceptual explanation, this information also includes fascinating glimpses into little known aspects of the topic that will enhance

> *The Science and Engineering Practices give students the opportunity to assume the role of scientists through activities correlated to each topic.*

your science literacy as students are building theirs through the writing prompts.

The Science and Engineering Practices give students the opportunity to assume the role of scientists through activities correlated to each topic. Whether evaluating information or conducting research, they use the same strategies that actual scientists use in their search for answers and solutions.

The Writers/Teachers Behind *Take 5! for Science:*

Kaye Hagler

How do we know the *Take 5!* strategy works? For years I have used quick writes to support my students' thinking, "exercising their brain muscles" as I would tell them. Each day would begin with a critical thinking prompt that would quickly capture their interest and engage them in pondering the possibilities. The evidence of their success was not only in the range of thinking I encountered in their writing, but also in their standardized test scores where they were required to address unknown prompts. The proof has also come from many of the thousands of teachers who have incorporated *Take 5!* into their own classrooms and from professional development coordinators who have acknowledged its value as a means for developing critical thinking, which in turn has led to more insightful writing opportunities. The daily routine of writing in just those first few minutes of class has shown itself to be a key component in helping to raise student achievement in writing across the curriculum. In this new work, *Take 5! for Science*, I hope all students will be pulled into the world of scientific possibilities through the Explore and Dig Deeper prompts.

Judy Elgin Jensen

As a former science teacher and now a full-time writer of science resources, I'm here for the science. The science teacher in me has advocated the idea of "scientific literacy" from the beginning of my instructional years. How do we develop a scientifically literate society? Start early. Engaging students in writing about science ideas, concepts, processes, and wonderings gives them a way to express both understanding of the topic and creativity in how they do so. It makes their thinking visible and gives them (and you) a tool for evaluating misconceptions or disconnects in their thinking. Students' application of science and engineering practices goes far beyond the idea of skills and gives them real insight into how scientists and engineers actually go about their work. Both give students the comfort that science is neither mysterious nor difficult to grasp, which paves the way to scientific literacy in adulthood.

The Objectives of *Take 5! for Science*

As educators, we know the concerns and issues facing teachers today. Among those is a mandate for "standards-based" lesson plans. Often, we hear teachers lament the loss of the fun, engaging activities used in the past. These activities are placed on a shelf in the back of the closet because of time constraints. For that reason, four main objectives stand behind this educational resource.

> Objective #1: Promote engagement—bringing students to the table or desk for a quick burst of critical thinking.
>
> Objective #2: Incorporate writing into each science topic.
>
> Objective #3: Assist teachers by aligning each prompt with the standards.
>
> Objective #4: Provide daily practice in responding to a prompt in a timed-response environment.

The Standards Used for *Take 5! for Science* Prompts

The Next Generation Science Standards (NGSS) provide the framework for *Take 5*'s "Science Information" and "Science and Engineering Practices" components. The NGSS were developed in a process initiated by The National Research Council (NRC) of the National Academy of Sciences, the National Science Teachers Association (NSTA), the American Association for the Advancement of Science (AAAS), and Achieve, a nonprofit education reform organization dedicated to developing college and career readiness skills. With direct input from 26 lead state

*The Next Generation Science Standards (NGSS) provide the framework for **Take 5's** "Science Information" and "Science and Engineering Practices" components.*

partners and responses from two drafts for public review, the NGSS were finalized for adoption in the spring of 2013. Previous national science standards were approximately 15 years old, a major lapse of time in the science world when advanced technology and scientific discoveries reveal previously uncharted opportunities for learning. These current standards also incorporate STEM (science, technology, engineering, and mathematics) practices into each topic. If your school system does not currently utilize NGSS, you will discover how easily the prompts connect with your state or local standards by using, as an umbrella, specific topics from the three main branches of science: Earth, Life, and Physical.

Key Components of NGSS in *Take 5! for Science*

The NGSS detail examples of performance expectations that incorporate science and engineering practices, disciplinary core ideas (DCIs), and crosscutting concepts. *The Take 5!* approach focuses on a disciplinary core idea and the science and engineering practices. The DCIs are listed at the beginning of each topic. The first DCI listed is for the Explore level. These are typically geared toward K–2 students, but you might find them useful for students at other grade levels. Listed next is the Dig Deeper DCI, taken from the 3–5 level. Again, you have the flexibility to use these with any students to match their demonstrated abilities.

A typical DCI notation might look like this: **K-PS2.A**

K: Kindergarten (grade level)

PS: Physical Science (domain, or science discipline)

2: Core Idea (Motion and Stability: Forces and Interaction)

A: Component Idea (Forces and Motion)

In the NGSS, this code is followed by a description of the content included (in the above case: Pushes and pulls can have different strengths and directions). All PS2 DCIs will cover content related to Motion and Stability: Forces and Interactions no matter the grade level.

A copy of the NGSS is downloadable at nextgenscience.org. Choose the DCI arrangement for a copy that organizes the standards by grade level and DCI. This will give you easy access to the specific description of the content of each component.

Disciplinary Core Ideas

Disciplinary core ideas reflect the science content of the NGSS. According to the NGSS, a core idea must meet at least two criteria as outlined below (Next Generation Science Standards, 2011):

- ✓ Have broad importance across multiple sciences or engineering disciplines or be a key organizing concept of a single discipline;
- ✓ Provide a key tool for understanding or investigating more complex ideas and for solving problems;
- ✓ Relate to the interests and life experiences of students or be connected to societal or personal concerns that require scientific or technological knowledge; and/or
- ✓ Be teachable and learnable over multiple grades at increasing levels of depth and sophistication.

Science and Engineering Practices

The science and engineering practices model the behavior of a working scientist through such practices as questioning and investigating. "The NRC uses the term *practices* instead of a term like 'skills' to emphasize that engaging in scientific investigation requires not only skill but also knowledge that is specific to each practice." (Next Generation Science Standards, 2011) The NGSS highlight eight Science and Engineering Practices:

- ✓ Asking questions (for science) and defining problems (for engineering)
- ✓ Developing and using models
- ✓ Planning and carrying out investigations
- ✓ Analyzing and interpreting data
- ✓ Using mathematics and computational thinking
- ✓ Constructing explanations (for science) and designing solutions (for engineering)

✓ Engaging in argument from evidence

✓ Obtaining, evaluating, and communicating information (NGSS Appendix F, 2013)

Common Core State Standards in *Take 5! for Science*

This book focuses on science, yet each prompt is aligned with a Common Core State Standard (CCSS) for English Language Arts (ELA). This alignment is propelled by pedagogical shifts that are based on: 1) a national emphasis on incorporating writing and critical-thinking skills into the science curriculum and 2) research that underscores the integration of these areas in producing and extending scientific investigation, reasoning, and writing skills. Asking questions, planning and conducting simple experiments, making observations, organizing, communicating, describing, comparing, and explaining are all processes that allow for integration.

The ability to respond to a prompt is becoming increasingly important in today's educational climate. From the classroom to standardized tests, science competitions, and even scholarship applications, the writing prompt is becoming a required tool, and thus a skill to be mastered. Per the National Governors Association Center for Best Practices (2010), "Students need to learn to use writing as a way of offering and supporting opinions, demonstrating understanding of the subjects they are studying, and conveying real and imagined experiences and events. They learn to appreciate that a key purpose of writing is to communicate clearly to an external, sometimes unfamiliar audience, and they begin to adapt the form and content of their writing to accomplish a particular task and purpose . . . [.] To meet these goals, students must devote significant time and effort to writing, producing numerous pieces over short and extended time frames throughout the year."

A daily routine of writing not only increases a student's ability to pull ideas together in an increasingly competent manner, but it also helps to reduce the anxiety that accompanies such tasks. If it begins in the primary grades, writing ability only improves as it is reinforced in the upper grades. The "Range of Writing" standard (10), applicable to all prompts, is: "Write routinely over extended time frames (time for research, reflection, and revision) and shorter time frames (a single sitting or a day or two) for a range of tasks, purposes, and audiences."

Just as the *Take 5! for Language Arts* prompts provided opportunities for developing critical-thinking and writing skills, *Take 5! for Science* incorporates those skills and much more with its focus on science topics and standards. More and more curriculum programs are moving toward an integration of these two disciplines: science and writing. While not all school systems may incorporate NGSS or CCSS, the standards used in *Take 5!* align well with other state standards that focus on claims and evidence, informative and narrative writing, information gathering, and vocabulary building.

Integration of Science and Writing: Endorsed by Research

Traditionally, writing in the science discipline has been limited to the development of lab reports and research assignments that, according to McComas (1998), use such headings as "purpose, methods, observation, and conclusions. This traditional format has been challenged as a 'myth' for modeling authentic practices of scientists." (Fazio and Gallagher, 2009).

Current thought recognizes the limitations of such writings in widening the range and purpose of writing opportunities not only in the modern day science classroom but for college- and career-readiness as well. In addition, proponents of science literacy advocate instruction on writing strategies from a student's earliest brush with science in the elementary classroom to foster an understanding of basic scientific terms and principles. "Students translate the science language into an everyday form of language that they can understand for themselves. They then translate the meaning . . . into an audience language to provide meaning and explanation for their audience" (Jang, 2011).

Innovative educators have discovered the gains in moving writing into all disciplines as it becomes the stimulus for critical thought. The skill of writing to develop a finished body of work then becomes writing to develop knowledge whatever the subject may be (Troia, Shankland, and Heintz, 2010).

Still another advantage for incorporating scientific inquiry, even at the preschool level, is the early introduction of scientific terms into the child's vocabulary, using terms that children can understand. You might say, for example, that some animals travel great distances to find food. They "migrate." "New words and their meanings are likely to be learnt as the child experiences new concepts and semantic demands" (Thurston, Grant, and Topping, 2006). Innovative educators have discovered the gains in moving writing into all disciplines as it becomes the stimulus for critical thought.

Other studies also found "investigative activity" produced gains in learner outcomes because the activities activate prior knowledge. The prompts in *Take 5!* undertake complex topics, such as photosynthesis, by paring them down to a task or making analogies that will later build on a more complete understanding of the topic. They also introduce essential scientific terminology along the way. While the term *photosynthesis* might sound like a foreign language to a first grader, the concept of a plant having its own factory or grocery store to make its own food is a concept that young learners can easily grasp. Informal activities, such as responding to a given prompt, promote reasoning and intuition as starting points for developing critical thinking and reflection in science (Coffey, Douglas, and Stearns, 2008).

While they may not have a grasp of writing and sentence structure, preschool students can still respond to prompts by putting their ideas into drawings. Whether they are asked to explain how something works, make predictions, tell a story, or provide a claim, young students can visualize their thinking in each response. Connecting writing and science allows students to connect their life world with the world of science (Fazio and Gallagher, 2009).

Chapter 1: Getting Started

The quick write method of writing provides the foundation for each prompt in *Take 5! for Science*. Your science curriculum can be enhanced by these daily prompts because each one

- engages students in the first minutes of class with a curriculum-based topic of study,
- promotes critical thinking and reflection,
- incorporates writing into the main branches of science,
- integrates science-based terminology into student writing,
- represents operational thinking,
- prompts students to seek solutions to problems and evidence for claims, and
- activates prior knowledge.

As with *Take 5! for Language Arts*, prompts are not "fluff" activities. Instead, they meet important objectives for learning as each is

- an introduction to each day's lesson;
- a means to develop ideas for ongoing discussions about a topic under study;
- an assessment of growth, though informally, using the collective body of work;
- an engaging activity that meets rigorous standards; and
- an opportunity for developing collaborative learning experiences when used in pair or team learning settings.

What's Inside a Typical *Take 5!* Topic?

- **The Heading:** This provides the Language Link, Learning Setting, and Topic.
- **Prompt Supplies:** Some prompts or activities require specific materials, and we have listed the materials on the Teacher Page. Assemble these materials so that they are ready for the students as soon as they walk into the classroom. Place them in a basket for the students to retrieve or on each student's desk, depending on the time and space available.
- **Disciplinary Core Ideas from the NGSS**
- **CCSS ELA Standards**
- **Background Science Information**
- **Science and Engineering Practices**
- **Additional Resources** (websites and books): Many of the additional resources suggest search terms for the Internet, while others show specific links. These links were operational at the time of the publishing of this book.
- **Prompts** (Explore and Dig Deeper)

Using the Background Science Information

Refresh your understanding of key science concepts and processes for confidence in facilitating discussions and evaluating student understanding. This section will also alert you to common misconceptions, give you some interesting data to share, and help you link science to other topics under study.

Facilitating Science and Engineering Practices

Most of the suggestions promote minds-on action. When materials are needed for hands-on stimulus, the materials are included here.

Displaying the Prompt

The prompts may be displayed in a variety of ways. You might project the prompt with a document camera or overhead projector so students see it as they arrive in the classroom. You can also copy the prompt and place into students' folders or scan the prompts to display on an interactive whiteboard. You may also choose to select student volunteers to read aloud the prompt.

Responding to Each Prompt: The Science Notebook

In *Take 5! for Science*, we suggest that students use a Science Notebook to respond to prompts. Using a Science Notebook helps foster the language of science. In addition to expanding their science vocabularies, students will activate inquiry-based learning through a variety of writing opportunities (informative, narrative, opinion, claims and supporting evidence, to name a few). Often, students supplement their written communication with drawings.

Current research supports the practice of using Science Notebooks: "Students as early as kindergarten should be encouraged to keep a record of science investigations. Often these entries will come in the form of scribbles or drawings only decipherable to the student yet serving as the foundation for more advanced inquiry and response" (Klentschy, 2008). The Science Notebook is therefore viewed as a valid learning tool to help students explain, describe, and integrate new information. (Coffey et al., 2008)

What Goes into the Science Notebook?

While individual teachers have their own specifications, some basic criteria could include the following:

- ✓ the date in the upper left or right position on the page,
- ✓ the topic of the prompt (i.e., *Force, Hibernation*), and the response itself.

Examples of other types of information that could be included in the Science Notebook:

✓ a list of student-formulated questions, based on the topic
✓ clippings from a newspaper, magazine, or Internet source about new findings on the specific topic under study
✓ an ongoing vocabulary list of terms encountered in the three branches of science studied
✓ student-developed foldable organizers

What Kinds of Science Notebooks Work Best?

Most students will use traditional composition or spiral notebooks. Since students will often use their notebooks away from a desk or table, be sure notebooks are easily transportable and can stand alone as opposed to incorporating them into a thick binder. The form, however, is less important than the content. For that reason, the Science Notebook can be simply a stack of notebook paper bound with a construction paper cover that is covered with science-related terms. (You could prompt students to draw a collage of science images on the cover that represents their current knowledge of the three branches of science: Earth, Life, and Physical.) Other students might prefer a folder on the computer where they can store documents. Despite the format, each entry provides opportunities for constructing meaning from a given situation through open-ended responses. In addition, the Science Notebook expands students' vocabulary with each term under discussion.

How Should Notebooks Be Assessed?

Gone are the days when teachers would subject themselves to mountains of spiral notebooks piled high. Today, you can observe student learning via student responses in an informal environment. Use the Science Notebook as evidence in this process. For grading purposes, a simple rubric like the samples provided on the next few pages can do the job. One of the rubrics is learner-centered, while the other is written from an educator's point of view. Adapt the rubrics as needed to gauge students' science understanding. For younger students, for example, you might simply provide a checklist with statements to which students can agree or disagree, such as "I included facts about science" and "My drawings have science details."

Additionally, be sure to devote a few extra minutes for student reflections at the end of the response time as these can encourage meaningful discussions on the topic. Most students love to share what they have written. Others will slowly come around as the year progresses. These discussions help to create the transition into that day's lessons. As students share their ideas with their classmates, other ideas might surface as springboards for later investigation. It also cues you into what may need to be reexamined, clarified, or encouraged.

Take 5! for Science Rubric

EXAMPLE #1

My Science Notebook Rubric   Name: _____

	1	2	3
Science Content	My written responses demonstrate that I understand the science concepts. I can accurately use science terms in my writing.	My written responses demonstrate that I understand some of the science concepts. I can accurately use some of the science terms in my writing.	My written responses demonstrate that I understand a few of the science concepts. I can use a few of the science terms in my writing.
Drawings	My drawings are accurately labeled and include all the important details.	I labeled most of the parts of my drawing, and I included some details.	My drawings are very small. I did not include details or labels.
Organization	I have dated all my entries. They are in the correct order.	I dated most of my entries, and they are in the correct order.	I have dated few of my entries. The Science Notebook is not organized enough to follow it.

Take 5! for Science Rubric

EXAMPLE #2

Science Notebook Rubric		Student Name: _____	
4	**3**	**2**	**1**
Key science terms are used and convey accurate meanings.	Key science terms are used and most convey accurate meanings.	Some key science terms are used that convey accurate meanings.	No key science terms used, or terms do not convey accurate meanings.
Synthesis of concepts demonstrates a clear and accurate understanding of science ideas.	Synthesis of concepts demonstrates a reasonable understanding of science ideas.	Synthesis of concepts demonstrates some understanding of science ideas.	Synthesis of concepts presented demonstrates no understanding of science ideas.
Logic behind synthesis, analysis, or evaluation of science ideas is well developed in all aspects.	Logic behind synthesis, analysis, or evaluation of science ideas is developed in most aspects.	Logic behind synthesis, analysis, or evaluation of science ideas is developed in few aspects.	Logic behind synthesis, analysis, or evaluation of science ideas is poorly or not developed.
Claims are all supported by factual evidence.	Claims are mostly supported by factual evidence.	Claims are supported by some factual evidence.	Claims are not supported by factual evidence.

Index of Topics and Titles

Clouds

Water Cycle

Sun

Glaciers

Seasons

Types of Rocks

Volcanoes

Erosion

Climate

People and Earth

Tornadoes

Earth as a System

Landforms

Wind

Day

Night

Oceans

Deposition

Galaxy

Precipitation

Fossil Fuels

Phases

Moon

Revolution

Stars

Shadows

Renewable Resources

Bodies of Water

Weathering

Rotation

Hurricane

Chapter 2:
Earth Science Prompts

LANGUAGE LINK		LEARNING SETTING
Explore:	Research	Collaboration
Dig Deeper:	Informative Writing	Pair

Earth as a System

Science Information

Our planet is one giant system composed of smaller subsystems: geosphere (the soil and rock of Earth), hydrosphere (all of Earth's water and ice), atmosphere (the gases that surround the planet), and biosphere (all of Earth's living things). These subsystems constantly interact. For example, volcanic ash moves into the atmosphere and can be carried to other continents where it affects living things. Landforms and oceans change air movement, creating conditions that influence the kinds of living things in any given area. Other planets are systems made up of subsystems as well. Geospheres and atmospheres are common, yet Mars is the only planet to show signs of a hydrosphere; and none, as yet, have shown signs of a biosphere.

Science and Engineering Practices: Asking Questions and Defining Problems

Provide groups with an assortment of pictures, magazines, and newspapers or access to nature photography on the Internet. Encourage students to pose questions about what they observe in images. Record the questions, helping students to frame them in such a way as to be answered through an experiment or research on the Internet. Guide students to understand that "which," what," and "how" questions can be investigated or researched. "Yes" or "no" questions result in dead ends.

EXPLORE
Visitors from Space!

Visitors from a faraway planet are circling planet Earth in a spaceship. They are gathering information on this planet. Photographs need to be included in this report. Guess what? You and your team are the visitors! You are from this faraway planet. Each of you will draw a picture of Earth. These are your "photos." Be sure to show water, land, and even blowing winds. The photos were not taken at the same time, however. Each person needs to show a different view of Earth. Some areas may even be dark. Staple the pictures together. Add a blank sheet to the top. As a team, write your report. What have your learned about Earth? Include the terms "water," "wind," and "land."

Ready? Take

DIG DEEPER
Planet Earth

A new video game is being developed. You and a partner are the project leaders. The game is called "Planet Earth: The Ultimate Trip." In this game, players travel across Earth visiting many of its different features—traveling over its surface, below its oceans, and even high into its atmosphere. As players land at specific locations, they must answer a question about Earth. An e-mail has just arrived. The company's supervisor of games needs an update on the project. In this update, she has asked for specific information:

- the objective of the game
- a sample location and a question that might be asked there
- a new element to add to the game to make it more appealing

The success of this project depends on you.

Ready? Take

The Cliffs of Moher

Science Notebook

Google Earth Map (Cliffs of Moher)

Photograph (Cliffs of Moher—page 14)

NGSS

2-ESSA.B: Plate Tectonics and Large-Scale System Interactions

4-ESS2.B: Plate Tectonics and Large-Scale System Interactions

CCSS

W.K.3, W.1.3, W.2.3: Imagined Event

W.3.8, W.4.8, W.5.8: Gather Information

ADDITIONAL RESOURCES

Examine photographs of different landforms around the world at websites, such as http://science. nationalgeographic.com/science/ earth/surface-of-the-earth/

Landforms by Lynn Van Gorp. Capstone: 2009. (5–6)

What Is a Landform? by Rebecca Rissman. Heinemann-Raintree: 2009. (PreK–1)

LANGUAGE LINK		LEARNING SETTING
Explore:	Narrative Writing	Collaboration
Dig Deeper:	Research	Individual

Landforms

Science Information

Maps are special kinds of models that Earth scientists use often. Broadly, maps use symbols to represent Earth's landforms, such as mountains, valleys, plains, plateaus, and bodies of water—both salt and fresh. Topographic maps and ones with specially coded keys may show how far above or below sea level a particular landform is. Certain maps eliminate the water to show landforms—mountains, valleys, volcanoes, and plateaus—that exist on the ocean floor as well. Maps don't have to be flat either. A globe is a kind of map. Even more simplistically, maps show the locations of things and what is around them. Maps that include scale relate the distance on the map to the actual distance on Earth.

Science and Engineering Practices: Analyzing and Interpreting Data

Conduct an Internet search for images using keywords, such as "plateaus landforms" or "hills landforms," and project several examples. Have students create operational definitions for the various landforms based on their observations. Optionally, you might use a global imaging map, such as Google Earth, to do a "flyover" of different regions of the country. The area around Denver, for example, will show plains and mountains.

Field Trip!

The class is going on a field trip. Everyone is so excited! Some want to go to the beach. Others want to visit the mountains, cliffs, and deserts. There are so many different landforms to see—even swamps with alligators! You and your team will draw a "Field Trip" map. Select four different landforms. Roll out the paper. Draw a road that starts at your present location. Curve the road along the map until it reaches the other end of the paper. Leave some room at the bottom. Now, it is time to go to work. Each person will draw one landform along the road trip. Label each landform.

Next, write the title "Coming Soon!" at the bottom of the map. Below the title, write two sentences about this adventure. What will the class be seeing and doing? Be very descriptive! Get the class excited!

DIG DEEPER

The Cliffs of Moher

Satellite image, maps, and photographs can bring faraway places into your home. You don't even have to pack a suitcase. People love to share photographs and tell all they have seen. But these observations are seen through someone else's eyes. What do you see? Today, we will take a virtual trip to the famous Cliffs of Moher, located on the west coast of Ireland. Begin your visit at a global imaging map, such as Google Earth. Examine the landscape of this landform carefully. What can you learn about the cliffs from the digital globe? Write down at least two observations in bullet form. Next, study the photograph. Add two additional observations, also in bullet form. Use these brief notes to write a description of this famous landform.

Ready? Take

LANGUAGE LINK		LEARNING SETTING
Explore:	Opinion	Individual
Dig Deeper:	Narrative Writing	Individual

Bodies of Water

Science Information

Broadly, bodies of water are fresh (lakes and rivers), brackish (estuaries and some wetlands), or salty (oceans). The water in those bodies may circulate (as ocean currents do), flow from higher elevation to lower elevation (as rivers do), or have generally still water (as lakes do). Note that the name of a given body of water is more a matter of local custom than anything because, according to the United States Geological Survey (USGS), few rules apply for the generic names given to geographic features.

While aquifers are often described as "underground rivers," they are not free-flowing bodies of water. Groundwater collects in the spaces within rock itself or in the spaces between grains of sand or gravel. The layer becomes saturated with water. Water in aquifers can move from higher elevations to lower ones. The top of this water-saturated layer is called the water table, and it forms the surface of lakes and ponds.

Develop Science and Engineering Practices: Obtaining, Evaluating, and Communicating Information

Students might use county or state maps to identify various bodies of water near where they live and compare and contrast them. Is the local water body a pond, a lake, or perhaps a bog? Suggest they make a "bodies of water" brochure that gives data about each. Additional research could include why those bodies of water have the local names they do.

PROMPT SUPPLIES

What Lives in a Pond?	*Aquifer Kids*
Science Notebook	Science Notebook
Colored pencils	Colored pencils or create-your-own-comic-strip at websites, such as http://www.marvelkids.com

NGSS	CCSS
2-ESS2.C: The Roles of Water in Earth's Surface Processes	W.K.1, W.1.1, W.2.1: Support with Reasons
5-ESS2.C: The Roles of Water in Earth's Surface Processes	W.3.3, W.4.3, W.5.3: Event sequence

ADDITIONAL RESOURCES

The Environmental Protection Agency (EPA) provides an informative package of information and activities at http://www.epa.gov/ Search: "Magnificent Ground Water Connection"

Locate your area's local watershed at "Surf Your Watershed" at http://cfpub.epa.gov/surf/locate/index.cfm

Comparing Bodies of Water by Rebecca Rissman. Heinemann-Raintree: 2010. (PreK–1)

The World's Most Amazing Rivers by Anita Ganeri. Heinemann-Raintree: 2009. (3–5)

What Lives in a Pond?

Will you find a whale in a pond? No whales live in a pond. They live in the ocean.

Will you find an octopus in a lake? No octopus lives in a lake. They live in the ocean.

What lives in a freshwater pond?

Draw a picture of a pond. What lives in your pond?

Could there be tadpoles, frogs, ducks, fish, mosquitoes, or snails? Maybe an alligator lives there. What about beavers or dragonflies?

When you finish, turn your drawing over. List one living thing that could NOT live in this picture. Complete this sentence:

"A _____ could not live in a pond because _____."

Ready? Take 5!

©2016 Kaye Hagler and Judy Elgin Jensen from *Take 5! for Science*. This page may be reproduced for classroom use only.

Aquifer Kids

It's a fact!

*About 50–60 percent of our weight is composed of water.

*All vital organs depend on water to function.

So what does that mean? It means we need to drink water every day!

Where do we get water? No, not that plastic bottle or the water fountain. Go deeper!

Our drinking water is from surface water or groundwater. Surface water is from streams, rivers, and lakes. Groundwater is in the ground! Water collects in underground rock layers and sand. These watery layers are called "aquifers." These water sources need to be protected. Who can help? The Aquifer Kids! Create an adventure for these young, water-protecting superheroes. Divide your paper into four equal squares, called panes. Use balloons for dialogue. Somewhere in this dialogue include the following terms: "groundwater," "lakes," "streams," "aquifer," and "freshwater."

Ready? Take 5!

NGSS

NGSS	CCSS
2-ESS2.C: The Roles of Water in Earth's Surface Processes	W.K.1, W.1.1, W.2.1: Claim and Support
5-ESS2.C: The Roles of Water in Earth's Surface Processes	W.K.3, W.1.3, W.2.3: Myths W.3.1.B, W.4.1.B, W.5.1.B: Claim and Support

ADDITIONAL RESOURCES

Watch a video of the thriving world beneath the ocean's surface, such as http://video.nationalgeographic.com/video/why-ocean-matters

Just imagine a 40-story mountain of salt! Discover this and more in "The Ocean" by Kathy Kranking at http://www.nwf.org/Kids/Ranger-Rick/Animals/Mixture-of-Species/Ocean-Animals.aspx

Deep Oceans by Ellen Labrecque. Heinemann-Raintree: 2014. (1–3)

Why Is the Sea Salty?: And Other Questions about Oceans by Benjamin Richmond: Sterling Children's Books, 2014. (K–3)

LANGUAGE LINK		LEARNING SETTING
Explore:	Opinion/Narrative	Pair
Dig Deeper:	Opinion	Individual

Oceans

Science Information

Water covers about 70 percent of Earth's surface, and almost all of that water is found in the global ocean—the interconnected Atlantic, Pacific, Indian, Arctic, and Southern (or Antarctic) Oceans. On average, salts make up about 3.5 percent of ocean water, while salts make up less than 0.5 percent of freshwater.

Most animals have special mechanisms for dealing with excess salt because too much salt in the body causes water to move out of the cells and the body to dehydrate. Marine animals may have special salt glands while in humans the kidneys flush out salts.

Where do the oceans' salts come from? Mostly from the land. Although different cultures give varied explanations in folktales and mythology, the erosion of minerals by freshwater streams and rivers dumps salts into the oceans. Underwater volcanoes and hydrothermal vents spew salts into the water as well. Over time, the salts have become concentrated, because they do not evaporate when water evaporates from the oceans.

Develop Science and Engineering Practices: Planning and Carrying Out Investigations

Help students visualize how the amount of salts in the oceans compares with the amount in freshwater and that salts do not evaporate. Add one cup of tap water to each of two shallow pans. Label one pan "freshwater." Add one heaping tablespoon of salt to the second pan and stir until it dissolves. Label it "salt water." Set the pans where they will not be disturbed. Check two to three times a day until both pans appear to be empty. Observe and record the results.

EXPLORE
Salty Tales

Drew is going to the beach. He has never seen an ocean! The water, waves, and sand are amazing! He runs into the water. Crash! A large wave knocks him down. Don't worry. He is fine, but he comes up sputtering. He takes a big gulp of water in his fall. Yuck! The water is so salty! He is glad his mom packed plenty of fresh water. People can't drink salt water. Drew begins to think about this. *Who or what put salt into the ocean?* He searches for an answer to this question. He asks two different people. He receives two completely different answers. First, he asks a scientist. Next, he asks his grandmother. She is wise, but she is known for spinning tall tales. How do they each respond? With a partner, write their responses to this question.

Ready? Take

DIG DEEPER
Ship Ahoy!

You are looking at a map of the world. Wow! There is so much blue! That's because oceans cover about 70 percent of Earth's surface. Lucky for you! You have always wanted to take a trip around the world. Now is your chance. Your sailboat is ready to go. Use the World Map to chart your course. Start at one point on the map, a port on an ocean. Draw arrows to show your direction of travel. On the back of the map, make a list of the different bodies of water you sailed through. List them in the order traveled. Then, consider this question. *Should separate names be given to each of the five main bodies of water, or should there be only one ocean name?* What is your opinion? Support it with specific reasons.

Ready? Take

Glacier Explorers | *Strange Scientist*

Science Notebook | Science Notebook

NGSS

2-ESS2.C: The Roles of Water in Earth's Surface Processes

5-ESS2.C: The Roles of Water in Earth's Surface Processes

CCSS

W.K.1, W.1.1, W.2.1: Support with Reasons

W.3.3, W.4.3, W.5.3: Develop Imagined Experiences

ADDITIONAL RESOURCES

What is happening to the world's glaciers? Learn more with this interview with a glaciologist at http://www.pbs.org Search: "Fastest glacier"

Take a virtual trip to the South Pole with live cams posted by different countries, such as at the websites http://www.esrl.noaa.gov/gmd/obop/spo/movies.html and http://www.antarctica.gov.au/webcams/mawson

Arctic Attack (from the Batman series) by Robert Greenberger. Heinemann-Raintree: 2010. (2–3)

Glaciers by Mari Schuh. Capstone, 2010. (K–1)

The South Pole by Nancy Dickmann. Heinemann-Raintree: 2013. (1–3)

LANGUAGE LINK		LEARNING SETTING
Explore:	Opinion	Individual
Dig Deeper:	Narrative Writing	Individual

Glaciers

Science Information

Glaciers form when more snow falls than melts in an area. As the snow piles up, it becomes denser and more packed—more like an ice cube than a snowflake. The weight of the glacier itself causes it to begin moving, and it acts like a slowly creeping frozen river. Like a liquid river, glaciers carry along sediments as they slowly scrape across the landscape, carving out uniquely shaped valleys. Ice sheets and ice caps are similar to glaciers but are larger and don't move.

In many ways, the thick ice of a glacier is a historical document that records the environmental conditions at the time the ice formed. As the snow falls, it traps dust, chemicals, and radioactivity. Bubbles of trapped air and materials form in the ice. Scientists use a hollow drill to extract long columns of ice. The various layers of ice and the bubbles they hold give evidence of past climates and other events on Earth.

Science and Engineering Practices: Analyzing and Interpreting Data

Have students examine the photograph of the Gap of Dunloe. Explain that this landform—a narrow mountain pass in Ireland—is a glaciated valley created thousands of years ago as flowing ice pushed through the area. How is the lake evidence that a glacier was once present? What other kinds of evidence would you look for in the area?

Glacier Explorers

You are standing on a glacier. Look around you. Ice glistens all around. The sun is shining, but it is still cold. It is time to hike back down. But first, you plant a pole into the ice. A flag is on the end. On this flag is your name and today's date. Exactly one year later, you hike the glacier again. Along the way, something catches your eye. It's your flag. The pole is still standing tall. But it isn't in the same spot. It is farther down. You grab your hiking journal. You can now answer two important questions.

- Why did the pole move?
- What can be learned from its current position?

....

Strange Scientist

Long ago, the Ancient Greeks used the suffix "-ology" to mean "the study of." The word "ice" in Latin is "glacies." Therefore, people who study glaciers are called glaciologists. Glaciers are slow-moving rivers of ice. Suppose you are a glaciologist who has been studying glaciers. One of your tools drills into the ice on a glacier and pulls out sections of ice called "cores." An ice core provides clues to any changes in the climate around Earth. You never know what an ice core might reveal! Measuring a core can tell you if the ice is thinning. You pull out a core and measure it. Now this is really interesting! You have discovered a startling new chapter in the history of this glacier. What have you found and what does it tell you? Include the terms "climate" and "glacier" in your answer.

....

Types of Rocks

Science Information

Rocks fall into three general categories based on where they form. Igneous rocks form from magma—molten rock from deep underground. Sedimentary rocks originate from sand, pebbles, and other broken-down materials that are cemented together. These are the most common of all rocks and can contain fossils. Metamorphic rocks form deep within Earth where extreme heat and pressure cause a complete change from their original form of either igneous or sedimentary.

Like water, the rock of Earth continually changes through a cycle—the rock cycle—though it takes millions of years to do so. Igneous or metamorphic rock on or near Earth's surface can be weathered into sedimentary. All types of rocks can move to Earth's interior as Earth's plates move where the ice melts and changes form.

Science and Engineering Practices: Using Mathematics and Computational Thinking

Draw a simple rock cycle diagram with the terms "igneous," "metamorphic," and "sedimentary" (in any order) in a triangle. Connect the terms with arrows going in both directions to create a cycle. Point out that the arrows show that sedimentary rock, for example, can become either igneous rock or metamorphic rock. Have them compare that to the words and arrows diagrammed in a straight line.

Guide them to understand that the cycle format eliminates the "beginning and end" implied by the straight-line format.

PROMPT SUPPLIES

Let's Rock!	*Moon Rocks*
Science Notebook	Science Notebook
An assortment of rocks	
Colored pencils or markers	

NGSS	CCSS
2-ESS1.C: The History of Planet Earth	L.K.5.A, L.1.5.A, L.1.2.5.A: Sorting
4-ESS1.C: The History of Planet Earth	W.3.3, W.4.3, W.5.3: Imagined Experience

ADDITIONAL RESOURCES

Discover more about how rocks and minerals are formed at websites, such as http://www.pbslearningmedia. org Search: "Rocks and Minerals"

How does the rock cycle on the moon differ from that on Earth? Find out at websites, such as http://nasa.gov/ Search: "Our World: The Rock Cycle"

Watch a video about the rock cycle, such as MIT's engaging "Rock Cycle" at http://video.mit. edu/watch/rock-cycle-13017/

Investigating Rocks: The Rock Cycle by Will Hurd. Heinemann-Raintree: 2009. (3–6)

Learning About Rocks by Mari Schuh. Capstone: 2012. (K–1)

Let's Rock!

Walking along a stream, Juan and Carolina found two strange rocks. At first, they thought they were alike. They were the same shape. Then they looked closely at the rocks. They looked at the colors. They rubbed their fingers across them. Guess what? They felt different. Now it's your turn to examine a rock. Choose one rock. Look at it carefully.

Write "My Rock" at the top of your page. Next, describe your rock. Use specific adjectives.

- What colors do you see?
- Does it have stripes, speckles, or other patterns?
- What is its texture? Is it rough or smooth?

Next, draw your rock. Add labels and a caption to your picture. Use your observations as a guide.

....

Ready? Take

Moon Rocks

Astronauts from six Apollo missions between 1969 and 1972 brought back more than 800 pounds (363 kilograms) of rocks from the moon. These rocks helped answer questions about the moon: Did it once hold life? How did the rocks form? Why are they all igneous rocks? People were fascinated with the moon rocks. Later, they were displayed at schools and museums. Oops! One rock accidentally fell out of the display case. Now it is about to go on a journey quite unlike its life on the moon. What happens next to the rock? Complete the story by taking the moon rock through a complete rock cycle. Where does it go next and how? What happens to the rock there? Ready to continue the moon rock adventures?

Ready? Take

Sand Castle

Science
Notebook

The Egyptian Pyramids

Science
Notebook

NGSS

2-ESS2.A: Earth
Materials and
Systems

4-ESS2.A: Earth
Materials and
Systems

CCSS

SL.K.5, SL.1.5,
SL2.5: Clarify
Ideas

W.3.2.B, W.4.2.B,
W.5.2.B: Support
with Facts

ADDITIONAL RESOURCES

View a series of photographs
of erosion at http://www.
nationalgeographic.com/
Search: "Erosion"

Landslides and the danger they pose
for those living in Hawaii can be seen
at http://www.pbslearningmedia.
org/ Search: "Water Erosion"

Living Beside the Ocean by
Ellen Labrecque. Heinemann-
Raintree: 2015. (1–3)

LANGUAGE LINK		LEARNING SETTING
Explore:	Presentation	Individual
Dig Deeper:	Informative Writing	Individual

Weathering, Erosion, and Deposition

Science Information

Weathering is the breakdown of Earth's materials. That breakdown
can occur through chemical means, such as when water seeps
through limestone and dissolves it, slowly creating a cave.
Mechanical means, such as when plant roots break through rocks,
can cause weathering as well. Erosion is the movement of sediments
from one place to another—what happens after weathering occurs.
Erosion creates shifting sand dunes and wears down mountains.
Deposition is the laying down of sediments carried by the wind or
water. Deltas form through deposition. Weathering, erosion, and
deposition go hand in hand, but they are not the same thing.

Science and Engineering Practices: Constructing Explanations and Designing Solutions

Encourage students to record evidence they observe of weathering,
erosion, or deposition around the school or elsewhere in the
community. Evidence might include a broken sidewalk near a tree
(weathering), a muddy trail washed across the playground (erosion),
or a pile of materials at the mouth of a downspout (deposition).
Encourage students to construct explanations for what happened
using their evidence.

EXPLORE
Sand Castle

It's time to go to the beach! Do you have everything? Beach towel? Sunscreen? Beach toys? Along the shore, you and your friends work all day to build a giant sand castle. It has tall towers and a bridge to cross a moat. Oh no! You have a problem.

The castle is built too close to the water's edge. Erosion alert! The waves will lap at the walls. They will pull the sand away. The castle will then crash into the ocean. You need a solution to this problem. How can you stop erosion at least for the day? First, create a drawing of your plan. Next, explain why this plan might work.

Ready? Take

DIG DEEPER
The Egyptian Pyramids

You have been sent to investigate and report on damages caused to the famous pyramids of Egypt. These pyramids were built thousands of years ago. Today, however, they do not look quite the same. Some blame the tourists. As you investigate, you aren't so sure they are solely to blame. You note three important facts. These historic pyramids were built from large blocks of limestone and granite. Limestone is sedimentary rock. Second, they were built on a sandy plateau. The sand is so deep in some places that smaller pyramids might still be buried in this area. Your third observation is the force of the wind-driven sand. It can actually hurt if you aren't completely covered. Use your observations to write your report. Explain the roles that weathering, erosion, and deposition played in damaging the pyramids.

Ready? Take

PROMPT SUPPLIES

Shake It Up!

Science
Notebook

Shaky Myths

Science
Notebook

NGSS

K-ESS3.B: Natural
Hazards

3-ESS3.B,

4-ESS3-2: Natural
Hazards

CCSS

L.K.5.D, L.1.5.D,
L.2.5.B: Action
Verbs

W.3.3, W.4.3,
W.5.3: Narrative
Writing: Myths

ADDITIONAL RESOURCES

Almost every day a small earthquake
is occurring somewhere on
Earth. Find out what's shaking
in your part of the world at the
U.S. Geological Survey (usgs.
gov). Search: "earthquake"

Student investigators Claire and
Nisha explore earthquakes at
http://pbskids.org/dragonflytv/
show/earthquakes.html

Search for earthquake safety
tips at websites, such as http://
www.dropcoverholdon.org

Anatomy of an Earthquake by Renée
C. Rebman. Capstone: 2011. (5–9)

Earthquakes! by Renée Gray-
Wilburn. Capstone: 2012. (1–2)

LANGUAGE LINK		LEARNING SETTING
Explore:	Grammar & Usage	Individual
Dig Deeper:	Narrative Writing	Individual

Earthquakes

Science Information

Eyewitness accounts describe the sensation of an earthquake
as a light shaking motion, a rocking back and forth, or riding a
succession of small waves. Imagine what ancient people might have
thought was happening! Many constructed myths or stories to try
to explain it.

We now know that earthquakes occur when sections of Earth's
crust, called tectonic plates, push against, slip past, or move away
from one another, releasing energy in the form of waves. The waves
that radiate from the point where the slippage occurred continue
moving outward in all directions through the planet. (The point on
Earth's surface directly above this point is called the epicenter.) The
size of seismic waves reflects the strength of an earthquake, which
is indicated by a number on the Moment Magnitude Scale. On the
scale, larger numbers mean stronger earthquakes.

Science and Engineering Practices: Obtaining, Evaluating, and Communicating Information

Explain to students that most injuries during earthquakes occur
from falling or moving objects. Have students identify the
characteristics of a room in which it would be best to "Drop, Cover,
and Hold On." Model this activity by pointing out a potential
hazard, such as a tall bookshelf. Have them survey other classrooms
or their own homes and combine observations to determine
common hazards. Then have them use their observations to design
posters with the "Drop, Cover, and Hold On" theme.

Shake It Up!

It is getting so cold. Hurry! Bring your dog inside. Look at poor Scout. He is shivering. "Shiver" is an action verb. It means to move back and forth very quickly. You could also say Scout was shaking. That is another action verb. It means the same as "shiver." What about "quake"? That's right! "Quake" is also an action verb. It means the same as shiver and shake.

What about Earth? Can it shake or quake? Yes! That is called an earthquake! What can happen in an earthquake? Let's play Earthquake Connection. Make a list of many action verbs. Beside the verb, write or draw its connection to an earthquake.

Examples:

- Break–Glass will break.
- Duck–Duck under a sturdy object.

Let's get shaking!

DIG DEEPER
Shaky Myths

In mythology, the Greek god Poseidon ruled over the sea. He carried with him a trident. A trident is like a pitchfork. No one wanted to make Poseidon angry. If they did, he would raise his trident and strike the ground. This would cause the earth to shake, or quake. Here is another myth. This one is from Japan and involves a giant catfish called Namazu. He lives within the Earth and likes to cause trouble by shaking his tail. The only way he can be controlled is by the god Kashima who holds him down. But Kashima gets tired. Sometimes he relaxes a bit. When he does, Namazu shakes his tail and causes an earthquake. Now it is your turn. Create your own myth about what causes earthquakes. After that, explain how these mythical actions could represent real events.

Ready? Take

Volcanoes

Science Information

With a roar that sounds like a jet airplane, gas and lava spew out of a volcano. Glowing, molten rock flows down the sides, which is extremely dangerous because lava's temperature can be over 2,000°F (1,093°C) as it travels downhill from 6 to over 20 mph (9–32 kph). Everything it touches is destroyed. Other dangers include heavy ash falls (such as those that swallowed Pompeii), crushing falling stones, toxic fumes, and even tsunamis. Although the devastation is severe, the long-term effects to the soil lead to richness. Over time, the volcanic ash weathers into nutrient-rich soil that is well drained and easily tillable.

Science and Engineering Practices: Engaging in Argument from Evidence

Review the types of volcanoes, their dangers, and the safety procedures that are appropriate for your students. Students might then draw and label pictures about the dangers that result from volcanoes and how people can keep safe during one. Prompt further discussion with questions, such as the following:

- Why are volcanoes dangerous?

- How do volcanoes cause damage and destruction?

- How would you explain some ways to keep safe before, during, and after a volcano?

PROMPT SUPPLIES

Pop Rocks	*A Slow Burn*
Science Notebook	Science Notebook

NGSS

2-ESS1.C: The History of Planet Earth

4-ESS3.B: Natural Hazards

CCSS

W.K.3, W.1.3, W.2.3: Develop Imagined Experiences

W.3.1, W.4.1, W.5.1: Support with Reasons

ADDITIONAL RESOURCES

Students can create virtual volcanoes at websites, such as http://discoverykids.com/games/volcano-explorer/

View a video about the powerful effects of volcanoes at www.pbs.org Search: "Deadliest Volcanoes"

Volcano Explorers by Pam Rosenberg. Heinemann-Raintree: 2012. (1–2)

When Volcanoes Erupt by Nel Yomtov. Capstone: 2012. (3–4)

EXPLORE
Pop Rocks

Quick! Grab the binoculars. That may look like a tall mountain, but it's much more. It's a volcano. Hot gases, melting rock, and burning ashes are deep inside the volcano. These are trapped together, and it is getting hotter and hotter. Listen! Can you hear that roar? The volcano has just erupted! Don't worry. We are safe here. Look at the ashes spurting into the sky. We can also see the hot, melted rocks flowing down the sides of the volcano. This is called "lava." You have to call a friend! Describe this event and what you are seeing. Be sure to use the words "volcano," "erupt," and "lava."

....

Ready? Take

DIG DEEPER
A Slow Burn

Liquid, or molten, rock forms deep inside Earth. This is called "magma." After a volcano erupts, the molten rock flows down the sides of the volcano. Now, it is called "lava." As lava flows downward, it burns everything in its path. There is no stopping this deadly natural disaster. The fictional town of Pusatta lies in the shadow of Mt. Sreta, an active volcano. Over the last 100 years, Pusatta has experienced severe damage from four major eruptions. Each time the town rebuilds in the same location.

Many families farm the same fields tended by their ancestors. This is their home. Now, however, the town council has decided enough is enough. They have proposed moving the town 100 miles away. The original town and the surrounding area would be turned into a park with a science observatory station to monitor the active volcano. Many people are upset. They don't want to leave their homes. What would you do? Write a letter explaining who you are, where you stand on this issue, and why. Be very persuasive, using sound reasons. Be sure to include at least two scientific terms in your response.

....

Ready? Take

Water Cycle

Science Information

The water cycle is just that—the endless cycling of water from solid to liquid to gas and back again. Unlike new gases in the atmosphere, no new water is added to the amount of water on Earth. The water you are drinking today could have been in a stream where a T. rex once paused for a drink. The liquid water at the surface of lakes, rivers, and the ocean evaporates, or changes to a gas called water vapor. That happens when added energy from the sun causes the water molecules to move around more quickly. In the atmosphere, water vapor cools, and the molecules move more slowly. They come together and condense into tiny liquid water droplets that form clouds. As these droplets combine, they become heavy enough to fall to Earth's surface. If the temperature of the air through which they fall is below 32°F (0°C), sleet or snow falls. If the air is warmer, rain falls. The liquid and solid water on Earth's surface then evaporates again, continuing the cycle.

Science and Engineering Practices: Developing and Using Models

Guide students to model water cycle processes and observe the changes as they occur. Fill a small cup halfway with water. This represents the body of water (lake, ocean, or river). Carefully place the cup on the bottom of a plastic sandwich bag and seal the bag. Use duct tape to secure the bag to a sunny window (or position under an incandescent lightbulb). Be sure that the water does not spill from the cup. The energy from the sun (or lamp) will gradually cause the water to evaporate. It will then condense along the sides of the bag until falling back to the bottom of the bag as precipitation.

PROMPT SUPPLIES

Water World	Latin Lingo
Paper	Science Notebook
Colored pencils	
Easy-to-read chart of the water cycle	
Internet resources about the water cycle, such as "The Hydrologic Cycle" at http://www.srh.noaa.gov/jetstream/atmos/hydro.htm	

NGSS	CCSS
K-PS3.B: Conservation of Energy and Energy Transfer	W.K.3, W.1.3, W.2.3: Sequence
2-PS1.A: Structure and Properties of Matter	L.3.4.C, L.4.4.B, L.5.4.B: Root Words
5-ESS2.C: The Roles of Water in Earth's Surface Processes	W.3.2.C, W.4.2.C, W.5.2.C: Transitions

ADDITIONAL RESOURCES

Show a video about the water cycle, such as NASA's "Tour of the Water Cycle." This animated video shows the cycle using a single molecule of water at http://pmm.nasa.gov/education/videos/tour-water-cycle

Younger students might enjoy the video "Earth to Blorb: Water!" at http://pbskids.org/plumlanding/educators/context/114_earth_to_blorb_water.html

Inside the Water Cycle by William B. Rice. Capstone: 2010. (4–8)

Saving Water: The Water Cycle by Buffy Silverman. Capstone: 2009. (1–3)

EXPLORE
Water World

Imagine that you and your friends are going to a place called Water World! You will have so much fun at this water park. The park takes visitors on a wild ride along the water cycle. First, you float in a big pool of water.

Next, you are hit with a blast of hot air from a bright yellow sun overhead. Up you go!

The Evaporation Balloon takes you high into the air. Soon, you find yourself drifting high in the sky in a White Cloud.

What is the next ride? In the water cycle, water returns to Earth. It can be rain, snow, or ice. Draw the next ride in this theme park. Under the drawing, explain this ride.

Ready? Take

DIG DEEPER
Latin Lingo

Three key words in the water cycle are "evaporation," "condensation," and "precipitation." These three words come from the Latin language. In Latin, they look like this: "evaporatum," "condensare," and "praecipitatus." You are a word investigator, and you have learned the origins of each word.

- "Evaporatum" means "to draw off as vapor."
- "Condensare" means "to make dense."
- "Praecipitatus" means "to throw or fling down."

How do these early definitions relate to each step in the water cycle process? In your response, use linking words and phrases, such as "because of" and "since."

Ready? Take

Precipitation

Science Information

Precipitation is any kind of water that falls to Earth's surface—rain, snow, freezing rain, sleet, and hail. Within clouds, tiny liquid droplets move around and collide, causing them to become bigger and bigger. Finally the drops are large and heavy enough to fall to Earth's surface. The temperature of the air through which the drops fall determines whether the precipitation that reaches the ground is solid or liquid.

Hail is a bit unusual in that it forms within very tall storm clouds with strong updrafts. The drops are blown up into colder parts of the cloud, where they freeze. As they fall downward, they begin to melt. Then they are blown upward again to refreeze. This cycle repeats itself until the hailstone is too heavy to be blown upward and too large to melt, causing it to drop to the ground.

Science and Engineering Practices: Planning and Carrying Out Investigations

Spark investigative thought by asking, "How can you show that water in the air becomes a liquid as temperatures cool?" Present students with a list of materials or show them examples, such as a glass jar with a lid, ice cubes, liquid water, and a marker. Encourage them to describe how they might use the materials. For example, they could put the ice and water inside the glass, place the glass in a warm area, and observe the condensation (liquid water) on the outside. If they have marked the original level of the water and ice inside, it will be apparent that the liquid water did not "leak through" the glass but came from the air outside as it touched the cold glass.

PROMPT SUPPLIES

Flurry Worries	*Precipitation Symbols*
Science Notebook	Colored pencils or markers, pen
	World Map (page 190)

NGSS	CCSS
K-ESS2.D: Weather and Climate: Patterns	L.K.5.A, L.1.5.A, L.2.5.A: Word Relationships
3-ESS2.D: Weather and Climate: Predictions	W.3.4, W.4.4, W.5.4: Write for purpose and audience

ADDITIONAL RESOURCES

Check the weather in your area with a precipitation map, such as the one found at http://www.srh.noaa.gov/ridge2/RFC_Precip/

No two snowflakes are alike, according to Wilson A. Bentley, "The Snowflake Man" (1865–1931). He documented thousands of snowflake designs. Check out some of these intricate patterns in the Snowflake display at the Snowflake Bentley site http://snowflakebentley.com/museum2.htm

Snowflake Bentley by Jacqueline Briggs Martin. HMH Books for Young Readers: 2009. (K–3)

The Wettest Places on Earth by Martha E.H. Rustad. Capstone: 2010. (1–2)

Flurry Worries

Water falls to the ground. This is called "precipitation." It can come in the form of snow, ice, or rain. Too much precipitation can be a problem. Write about one problem.

Rain and snow are also very useful. Think of different ways to use them. Here is an idea. A big storm has knocked out the power. Pack a cooler with snow. Add juice bottles and milk cartons. The snow will help keep them cold. Write two forms of precipitation at the top of the page. Beneath each word, list different uses for each one. Here is another example. You can give your dog a bath in the rain.

....

Ready? Take

Precipitation Symbols

The weather service needs your help. Their weather maps must be updated. This is your task. Create a precipitation key for its maps. A key is a small box that explains symbols found on a map. Next, draw original symbols for rain, snow, sleet, and hail into a map key at the bottom of your weather map. Beside each symbol, list the form of precipitation.

Place these symbols around your map to show where and what forms of precipitation are taking place in the world. Circle one of these precipitation symbols on the map. In your notebook write a weather report for this circled area. Include information, such as amount of precipitation predicted, expected temperature, or any possible weather alerts. Are there any actions people should take as a precaution? Include that information as well.

....

Ready? Take

Clouds

Science Information

Clouds are collections of tiny water particles or ice crystals suspended in the air. The three main types of clouds are named by their appearance and the altitude at which they are located. Stratus and cumulus clouds are low clouds [< 6,500 feet (ft)/1,981 meters (m)]. Stratus clouds form in thick, gray layers and bring precipitation ranging from light rain to heavy rain or snow. Cumulus clouds look like cotton balls and can form vertical clumps. Cumulus clouds typically indicate fair weather, though tall ones can produce showers and thunderstorms. Cirrus clouds are found at higher levels (above 20,000 ft/6,100 m) and are delicate, wispy clouds that appear silky. They are formed almost entirely of ice crystals. Cirrus clouds are usually associated with clear, fine weather. Combinations of these base terms and other prefixes give more information about the kind of weather associated with clouds. "Alto" describes mid-level clouds. "Nimbo" refers to precipitation.

Science and Engineering Practices: Analyzing and Interpreting Data

Like scientists, students can also study patterns of weather using their knowledge of clouds. Work with students to maintain a classroom chart that shows the type of clouds on a given day, the temperature, and other weather conditions (wind, humidity, precipitation). Over time, encourage students to make a correlation between weather conditions and cloud types.

PROMPT SUPPLIES

The Stormy Canoe Trip	*Landscape Artist*
Science Notebook	Science Notebook
Cloud Chart, which can be found at http://www.crh.noaa.gov/. Search: "Cloud Classification and Characteristics"	Cloud Chart
	Colored pencils

NGSS	CCSS
K-ESS2.D: Weather and Climate	SL.K.5, SL.1.5, SL.2.5: Description
3-ESS2.D: Weather and Climate	SL.3.5, SL.4.5, SL5.5: Description

ADDITIONAL RESOURCES

Discover how famous art masterpieces depicted clouds at http:/www.windows2universe.org/ Search: "Clouds in Art"

Experience NovaLabs' "Cloud Lab" at the http://www.pbs.org/wgbh/nova/labs/lab/cloud/ Search: "Cloud Typing"

An innovative instruction in clouds can be found at http://www.pbslearningmedia.org/ Search: "Clouds and Weather"

How Does a Cloud Become a Thunderstorm? by Mike Graf. Heinemann-Raintree: 2010. (3–5)

Kit and Mateo Journey into the Clouds: Learning about Clouds by Cari Meister. Capstone: 2014. (K–2)

The Stormy Canoe Trip

"Let's push off!" the leader shouted. "Not a cloud in the sky. It is a good day for a canoe trip."

All the campers paddled in line behind the leader. Soon, a puffy, cotton ball cloud appeared.

"That's a cumulus cloud," the leader told them.

By afternoon, more clouds had gathered. One looked like a tall mountain of dark clouds.

"We better get to land," the leader shouted. "The clouds have changed. These show us a big storm is coming!"

Look at the different clouds on the cloud chart. Draw two boxes. Inside each box draw a different type of cloud. Above the box, write the name of the cloud. Below the box, describe the cloud and the weather. For example: Altocumulus. It looks like _____ (popcorn has spilled across the sky) and the weather is _____ (a nice day to be outside). After writing, present your description to a group.

Landscape Artist

You are an artist who enjoys creating landscapes. People really like your clouds. They look so real.

Use the Cloud Chart as a guide for your next masterpiece. It is a series of three drawings of the same simple scene. The only difference will be the clouds. The first drawing begins on a bright sunny day. Gradually, the weather changes in the second artwork. A major thunderstorm occurs in the last one. Check the chart. Which clouds will you use? Draw three boxes. In each box, create your landscape. Only the clouds will change in each scene.

Above each box, write the name of the cloud. Below each box, describe the connection between the clouds and the weather in each scene. Present your work to classmates when you are finished.

....

PROMPT SUPPLIES

Postcards from Home	*World Traveler*
Pencils, colored pencils, scissors, sheets of unlined paper	Science Notebook

NGSS

K-ESS2.D: Weather and Climate

3-ESS2.D: Weather and Climate

CCSS

SL.K.5, SL.1.5, SL2.5: Description

W.3.1, W.4.1, W.5.1: Evidence to Support Claim

ADDITIONAL RESOURCES

What's the difference between climate and weather? Have students use Internet resources to explore the answer to this question. Have them examine websites, such as http://www.nationalgeographic. com/ Type "Climate and Weather" in the video search box.

The Big Picture: Climate, a 4-book set by Louise Spilsbury, Angela Royston, Catherine Chambers, and Sarah Levete. Capstone: 2011. (1–3)

LANGUAGE LINK		LEARNING SETTING
Explore:	Presentation	Individual
Dig Deeper:	Opinion	Individual

Climate

Science Information

Although daily activities are influenced by the weather, it is a region's climate that determines the kinds of clothes people keep in their closets and the activities they look forward to doing at different times of the year. Climate is the average of weather conditions over a yearly cycle and is often described in qualitative terms, such as "mild" or "harsh." A region's climate depends on where the region is located within a continent and its proximity to large bodies of water and mountain ranges. Chicago's climate, for example, is influenced by the polar jet stream and would be colder in winter if not for the moderating effect of Lake Michigan. Although at a similar latitude, Portland's climate fluctuates less, is much wetter, and is generally milder because of its location between the Pacific Ocean and the Cascade Mountains. Travel over the Cascades to eastern Oregon and the climate is desert-like.

Science and Engineering Practices: Obtaining, Evaluating, and Communicating Information

Encourage students to discover more about the climate where they live. One such map can be found by typing "Climate Types for Kids" in a search engine, such as Google. Have volunteers locate your area and identify the climate. If you live in Florida, for instance, it is shaded orange—humid subtropical—at Google's climate map. Next, click on the climate type to learn more about the climate. Have students make a two-column chart and compare pertinent facts about their own climate and another. For younger students, organize the information as you click through it. Help students evaluate the information by comparing what they would wear in their home climate to what they would wear in the comparison climate.

Postcards from Home

The weather is always changing. It could be cold and rainy today. Tomorrow it might be sunny and warm. Climate is different. It does not change from day to day.

You and your family love to travel. This year you visited an island with a rain forest. It was very warm but often rainy. Next, you and your family visited a desert. Little rain fell there, and it was very dry and hot. During your trip, you sent two postcards to a friend. One was mailed from the island. The second was mailed from the desert. Fold a sheet of paper in half. Cut along the fold line. On one card, draw the island. On the other card, draw the desert. On the back of each postcard, describe the climate for each place.

....

Ready? Take

World Traveler

You are unhappy. Tomorrow is the last day of your visit to your grandmother's home. She is a world traveler with fascinating stories about the many places she has visited. With each story she tells, she pulls from her closet something she wore during each visit. Her clothing and accessories represent many different climates. Look closely. Based on what is hanging there, describe three different climates she has visited. Label each location (tropical paradise for example). As evidence, list some of the clothes and accessories (shoes, hats, etc.) that would have been worn there, and explain why.

....

Ready? Take

LANGUAGE LINK		LEARNING SETTING
Explore:	Informative Writing	Individual
Dig Deeper:	Informative Writing	Individual

Wind

Science Information

Wind is simply moving air caused by differences in air pressure within the atmosphere. Air moves from areas of high air pressure (shown by an "H" on a weather map) into areas of low air pressure (shown by an "L"). Wind is described by the direction from which it is blowing (a northern wind comes from the north) and its speed.

Globally, Earth's winds follow patterns. Between 0° and 30° north and south of the equator, rising warm air cools and moves westerly back toward the equator and are called "trade winds." Where the trade winds meet at the equator is an area with little air movement at the surface called the "doldrums." Winds between 30° and 60° move in the direction of the North and South Poles and are called "the prevailing westerlies." Air over the poles cools, sinks, and curves easterly forming "the polar easterlies."

Science and Engineering Practices: Engaging in Argument From Evidence

Provide an opportunity for students to observe and record local winds daily for a week. Have students draw pictures or write simple sentences that describe how strongly the wind is blowing. At the end of the week, challenge students to order the days by the strength of the wind. They should use their drawings or writings as evidence for their claim.

EXPLORE
See the Wind

Can we see the wind? Listen to or read the poem "Who Has Seen the Wind?" by Christina Rossetti. The poet says no, we cannot actually see the wind. Then how do we know it is there? We need proof! Draw a picture. In your picture, prove that the wind "is passing by." We need evidence, or details. Include two specific details as your evidence. The picture can be of a forest, a beach, or even a mountain. You pick the setting. Beneath your drawing, answer the question "How do we know the wind is there?" What details in your picture prove wind is present?

....

Ready? Take

DIG DEEPER
Wandering Winds

All across Earth, steady patterns of wind are taking place. With their sails unfurled, ancient ships would ply the waters from continent to continent. Why would early sailors need to know these wind patterns for long ocean crossings? Provide an example to support your answer. What about today? How could knowledge of wind patterns help another important activity? Explain.

....

Ready? Take

Hurricane Alert!   *Design a House*

Science
Notebook

Science
Notebook

Paper and pencil

NGSS

K-ESS3.B: Natural
Hazards

3-ESS3.B,
4-ESS3.B: Natural
Hazards

CCSS

W.2.2: Develop
Idea with Facts

W.3.2.A, W.4.2.A,
W.5.2.A: Aids in
Comprehension

ADDITIONAL RESOURCES

Have students search the Internet for
hurricane safety suggestions, such
as this brochure found at http://
www.nws.noaa.gov/os/hurricane/
resources/hurricane_safety.pdf

Hurricanes by Martha E.H. Rustad.
Capstone: 2014. (PreK–2)

Surviving Hurricanes by
Elizabeth Raum. Heinemann-
Raintree: 2012. (3–5)

*The Whirlwind World of
Hurricanes with Max Axiom,
Super Scientist* by Katherine
Krohn. Capstone: 2011. (3–4)

LANGUAGE LINK		LEARNING SETTING
Explore:	Informative Writing	Individual
Dig Deeper:	Informative Writing	Individual

Hurricanes

Science Information

Like blizzards, hurricanes occur more often in certain regions,
and people who live there take special precautions to reduce the
amount of hurricane damage. A hurricane is a huge, rotating low-
pressure system with winds that reach a minimum of 74 miles (119
kilometers) per hour. Hurricanes pose several threats. As the storm
approaches land, it pushes up the ocean water in front of it, causing
flooding from the surge in water levels. The system brings torrential
rains as well, which cause inland flooding and potential flooding of
communities downstream. As hurricanes become stronger, their
sustained winds might reach 150 miles (241 kilometers) per hour,
which not only blow structures over but also wildly fling debris
through walls and windows. Hurricanes can also spawn tornadoes.
Hurricanes traveling well off shore can still impact shorelines by
creating conditions that result in rip currents (extremely strong
currents) that move offshore and can drag swimmers away from
safety.

Develop Science and Engineering Practices: Using Mathematics and Computational Thinking

Guide students to conduct research on the Saffir-Simpson
Hurricane Wind Scale and its 1 to 5 rating based on a hurricane's
sustained wind speed. This scale estimates potential property
damage. After students research, have them illustrate each scale
rating with images collected on the Internet or with their own
drawings.

EXPLORE
Hurricane Alert!

A hurricane is coming! Emergency! This can be a dangerous situation. You are a weather forecaster. You must get the news out. First, draw a picture of a hurricane. Below it, explain the picture to viewers. Why is it dangerous? Then, help people prepare for the hurricane. What are two things they can do?

Ready? Take

DIG DEEPER
Design a House

You are a well-respected architect. A client wants to build a summer home along a beach in Florida. He knows, however, that hurricanes can cause severe damage. You need to design a home strong enough to withstand a powerful hurricane. There are two main dangers to homes during a hurricane: storm surges and wind damage. A storm surge is a wall of water pushed by wind that moves onto land. It causes beach erosion that can damage the foundation of a home. Strong winds are another problem. Loose items can be blown into windows. Even a Category 1 Hurricane (74–95 mi/hr or 119–153 km/hr) can rip shingles and tiles off of roofs. Trees can be uprooted and fall onto roofs, causing major damage. First, design your best, hurricane-proof home. Then, write a report to your client. Explain the home's special features.

Ready? Take

NGSS

K-ESS3.B: Natural Hazards

3-ESS3.B: Natural Hazards

CCSS

W.K.3, W.1.3, W.2.3: Transitional Devices

W.3.3, W.4.3, W.5.3: Sequential Order

ADDITIONAL RESOURCES

Have students view Internet videos about tornadoes and tornado safety, such as:

- Time For Kid's "TFK Tells You About Twisters" at http://www.timeforkids.com/photos-video/video/tfk-tells-you-about-twisters-152191

- Discovery Channel's "Life-Saving Chase" at http://www.discovery.com/tv-shows/storm-chasers/videos/life-saving-chase/

Anatomy of a Tornado by Terri Dougherty. Capstone: 2011. (5–9)

Surviving Tornadoes by Elizabeth Raum. Heinemann-Raintree: 2012. (3–5)

Tornadoes: Be Aware and Prepare by Martha E.H. Rustad. Capstone: 2015. (PreK–2)

LANGUAGE LINK		LEARNING SETTING
Explore:	Narrative Writing	Individual
Dig Deeper:	Narrative Writing	Individual

Tornadoes

Science Information

Tornadoes are rotating columns of air that drop down from a thunderstorm. Unlike hurricanes, they have no particular season but can occur at any time of the year. Their peak season, however, is March to October. The strength of a tornado is measured by its aftereffects, or how much damage it causes. The National Weather Service uses the EF-Scale (Enhanced Fujita Scale) to assign a damage scale to a tornado. An EF-5 would cause catastrophic damage. When conditions are favorable for tornadoes, a watch is issued. A warning means that a tornado has been sighted and people should take cover immediately.

Imagine chasing tornadoes in a fast-moving car. That is what storm chasers do to try to obtain more information on the formation and movement of tornadoes. While storm chasers are out in the field with the storms, storm spotters watch for conditions favorable to tornado formation and report that information to the National Weather Service.

Science and Engineering Practices: Developing and Using Models

The most damaging part of a tornado is the vortex, the center of the tornado. Here, the air moves rapidly, creating a strong force through a full rotation of air. To get a better idea of this vortex of rotating wind, you can create the rotating motion in this simple model. Fill an empty two-liter bottle three-fourths full of water. Add a few drops of liquid dish detergent. Put the cap on the bottle. Turn it upside down. As you hold it by the neck, spin the bottle in a circular motion. The faster the better! Now, stop. Watch carefully. Can you spot a small vortex in the water? Try this experiment again with different variations in the amount of water or detergent. You can also add glitter for a better view of the vortex.

EXPLORE
Super Storm

A big storm can bring wind and rain. Sometimes, the winds start spinning around. They pick up speed. The winds are moving faster and faster! Look! It looks like a funnel. Sometimes, this rotating funnel can hit the ground. This can be very dangerous. It is coming closer! What should you do? Use the words "first" and "then" in your answer.

....

Ready? Take

DIG DEEPER
Storm Chasers

Meteorological researchers discover and record weather patterns. Those who work in the field following storms are often called "storm chasers." In addition to collecting and interpreting data, they also prepare and broadcast weather conditions.

Today, you are a storm chaser. It has been a crazy day! So many things have happened. Your log is filled with a full day of tornado activity. Write at least one entry. Provide complete information so that others can follow your notes. First, include the day and the time of each event. Then, use the following subtopics for each entry:

Sighting: What did you see? Where did it occur?

Unusual formations or activity: What made this one different from others?

Action: What did you do?

....

Ready? Take

NGSS

K-ESS3.C: Human
Impacts on
Earth Systems

5-ESS3.C: Human
Impacts on
Earth Systems

CCSS

W.K.2, W.1.2,
W.2.2: Support
with Facts

W.3.2.A,
W.4.2.A,W.5.2.A:
Organization

ADDITIONAL RESOURCES

Have students search on the Internet
for articles about how kids can
impact the environment. They might
examine "Garbology by Joshua and
Sean" at http://www. pbskids.org/
dragonflytv/show/garbology.html

Students can play a game to
learn more about recycling,
reducing, and reusing at http://
www.kidsbegreen.org/

Bag in the Wind by Ted Kooser.
Candlewick Press: 2010. (K–3)

*Engineering an Awesome Recycling
Center with Max Axiom, Super
Scientist* by Nikole Brooks
Bethea. Capstone: 2013. (3–6)

Recycling: Reducing Waste by Buffy
Silverman. Capstone: 2008. (3–6)

LANGUAGE LINK		LEARNING SETTING
Explore:	Informative Writing	Individual
Dig Deeper:	Informative Writing	Pair

People and Earth

Science Information

The first Earth Day on April 22, 1970, was the beginning of an age
when "green" became a movement and not just a color. By the end
of that year on December 2, the Environmental Protection Agency
(EPA) was established. Today, it is globally recognized that our
practices have a wide-ranging impact on Earth and its resources,
with evidence of that impact on over 80 percent of Earth's surface.
Aluminum can recycling, for example, not only conserves metals
but also reduces the amount of water and fossil fuels used and the
amount of landfill space needed as well. It also negates the need for
continued mining. Individuals, groups, businesses, and governments
strive to protect Earth's resources and environments through the
choices they make. This idea of environmental stewardship is the
essence of Earth Day.

Science and Engineering Practices: Asking Questions and Defining Problems

Elicit from students their observations about how individuals, or
perhaps their class or school, impacts the environment. Then, using
their responses, guide them to ask questions they might investigate.
For example, how much used paper is the school recycling? Does
the schoolyard get watered and how often? Some of their questions
might lead to problems that can be solved, such as: How could
we make it easy for students to recycle used paper? Is there a way
to water the schoolyard with used water instead of tap water?
Students might then take the next step and plan how they would
answer the question or solve the problem.

Talking Trash

That hike made you so thirsty. Take a long drink from your water bottle. Now, return the bottle to your backpack. It can be **reused**. Reusing the bottle will help **reduce** trash. Trash piles will then get smaller and smaller. A soft drink can is not **reusable**. But it can be **recycled**. That means it can be used to make other objects. Our planet needs us to **reduce**, **reuse**, and **recycle**.

Draw three boxes. Label them *Reduce*, *Reuse*, and *Recycle*. In each box, draw a picture. The first box will show a way to reduce waste. The second box will show a way to reuse an object. The third box will show a way to recycle an object. Under the boxes, name one way to reduce, reuse, or recycle waste in your home.

Earth Day

It's Earth Day! Your hometown is holding a celebration to get everyone involved in protecting Earth and wisely using its resources. There will be exhibits, food, panel discussions, and games. You and your partner have been selected as chairpersons. What are your plans?

Make three columns. In the first column, list the name of each activity. The second column will describe the activity. The third column will explain its connection to Earth Day. Include at least two ideas. For example: a demonstration or speech by the local landfill supervisor.

Something New!

Science
Notebook

Power Up

Science
Notebook

NGSS

K-ESS3.C: Human
Impacts on
Earth Systems

4-ESS3.A: Natural
Resources

CCSS

W.K.2, W.1.2,
W.2.2: Support
with Facts

W.3.1, W.4.1,
W.5.1: Claim
and Evidence

ADDITIONAL RESOURCES

Search with students for Internet
resources about renewable energy,
such as Energy Kids (U.S. Energy
Information Administration
website) at http://www.eia.gov/
kids/energy.cfm?page=2

You can find various labs on the
Internet to deepen students'
understanding, such as those
at http://www.pbs.org/wgbh/
nova/labs/educators/

*A Refreshing Look at Renewable
Energy with Max Axiom, Super
Scientist* by Katherine Krohn.
Capstone: 2010. (3–4)

The Power of Energy by Rebecca
Weber. Capstone: 2011. (K–2)

LANGUAGE LINK		LEARNING SETTING
Explore:	Informative Writing	Individual
Dig Deeper:	Opinion	Individual

Renewable Resources

Science Information

Renewable resources are those that replenish themselves
continually, or within short periods of time. While people have used
the sun's energy to heat homes for centuries, it was the invention
of the solar calculator in 1978 that alerted the general public to
the ability to convert sunlight into electricity. Besides solar energy,
renewable resources include hydropower, geothermal, wind, and
biomass. Water stored behind a dam rushes through the base of
the dam to turn a generator to produce electricity, as does the
wind when it turns the blades of a windmill. Geothermal energy, or
heat from deep within Earth, creates steam that turns a generator.
Biomass, or leftover organic material, such as waste wood or
garbage, is usually burned to make steam to turn a generator as
well. Today, over half of renewable resources are used to produce
electricity, thus reducing the need for fossil fuels (petroleum,
natural gas, and coal), which are not renewable.

Science and Engineering Practices: Using Mathematics and Computational Thinking

Use the following data to give students practice in graphing and
interpreting what the graph means.

All energy resources: petroleum—36%, natural gas—27%,
coal—18%, renewable resources—9%, nuclear—8%

Renewable energy resources: biomass—49%, hydropower—30%,
wind—15%, geothermal—3%, solar—2%

You might develop the graph for younger children and ask
questions about it, while older students can create their own and
tell you what it means. Because of rounding of data, totals do not
add to 100.

Something New!

Mr. Jones is a tree farmer. He plants many trees. Fully grown trees are cut down. They will be used for many purposes. Mr. Jones then plants more trees in their place. Trees are a renewable energy source. The wind is also a renewable energy source. Have you ever seen a windmill or wind turbine? These use the wind's energy to create electricity. Imagine there's a wind turbine in your yard or on your roof. It provides clean energy for your home. But wait! The wind is not blowing today! Without the wind, what will you use for energy?

Complete this sentence: "I will use . . . because . . . ."

Is this a renewable resource? Why or why not?

Power Up

Mr. Tate placed solar panels on his home in Riverside, California. There is an abundant supply of energy from the sun where he lives. The town also operates a large wind farm to supply energy for the town. Both the sun and wind are natural resources that can be used over and over. They are called "renewable resources." You want your hometown to be more like Riverside, but the mayor refuses to discuss the issue. You are about to give a speech to the town council. Write your speech. Your claim is that the town needs to use more renewable resources. Provide your best, most convincing, evidence.

All Pumped Up!   *The Fossil Feud!*

Science
Notebook

Science
Notebook

Colored pencils

NGSS

K-ESS3.A: Natural
Resources

4-ESS3.A: Natural
Resources

CCSS

W.K.2, W.1.2,
W.2.2: Support
with Facts

W.3.1, W.4.1,
W.5.1: Support
with Reasons

ADDITIONAL RESOURCES

The Internet contains many
resources about fossil fuels that
students can find by searching.
They might examine:

- "What Are Fossil Fuels?
  - Definition, Advantages
  & Disadvantages" at
  http://study.com

- Bill Nye the Science Guy's
  "Fossil Fuels" video

*Buried Sunlight: How Fossil Fuels
Have Changed the Earth* by Molly
Bang, Penny Chisholm. The Blue
Sky Press: 2014. (PreK–3)

Fossil Fuels by Wendy Meshbesher,
Eve Hartman. Heinemann-
Raintree: 2010. (4–5)

LANGUAGE LINK		LEARNING SETTING
Explore:	Informative Writing	Individual
Dig Deeper:	Opinion	Individual

Fossil Fuels

Science Information

We use fossil fuels daily, even when we don't step foot in a car or
bus. The list is nearly endless when considering anything plastic,
nylon, or polyester, as well as varnishes, pesticides, aspirin, lipstick,
and countless other things. Fossil fuels—petroleum, natural gas,
and coal—formed from the remains of living things over 300 million
years ago. Oil and natural gas formed when aquatic organisms
were buried and then subjected to extreme heat and pressure. Coal
formed similarly, but from ancient trees, ferns, and other plants.
While fossil fuels are still forming today, they materialize so slowly
that the stores we have will eventually run out if use isn't reduced.

Science and Engineering Practices: Constructing Explanations and Designing Solutions

Millions of barrels of petroleum and natural gas are used annually
to make plastic products. All those fossil fuels for our plastic bottles!
What can we use instead of plastic? Students can work in groups,
making a list of all plastic items. Next, they could brainstorm
substitutes for as many items as possible.

EXPLORE
All Pumped Up!

We pump gasoline into our cars. Gas is a fuel. It burns and provides energy. This energy makes cars run. Gas comes from plants and animals that died long ago. Millions of years later, these dead plants and animals became fossil fuels—like gasoline! Draw a picture of a car. Beside it, draw a gasoline pump. Next, draw a very thick hose from the pump to the car. Do not shade or color the inside of the hose. Inside the hose draw tiny fish, plants, and small animals. Write the term "Fossil Fuels" above your picture. Below your picture, answer this question: "What is the connection between these objects and fuel?"

DIG DEEPER
The Fossil Feud!

In just one year, the United States used 134.5 billion gallons of gasoline. In another year, 191 million barrels of natural gas were used to produce plastic products. And yet, it took millions of years for prehistoric plants and animals to become the fossil fuels used today. Fossil fuels are currently the world's primary fuel source. Many people believe the world's supply of fossil fuels will soon be depleted, or used up. Others claim there are large quantities of fossil fuels in the earth. They state that new technology will eventually provide access to them as well. What do you think? What is your opinion on the use of fossil fuels? State your opinion, and provide at least two reasons to support it.

LANGUAGE LINK		LEARNING SETTING
Explore:	Research	Pair
Dig Deeper:	Opinion Writing	Individual

Galaxy

Science Information

On a cloudless night—should you be away from the light pollution of an urban area—you would be able to observe a faintly glowing band stretching across the night sky. You would see most of the roughly trillion stars of which the Milky Way Galaxy is comprised. These stars, and the gas and dust among them, are held together by gravity. They are too far away to be seen, however, other than as a faint glow. Greeks long ago created the word "galaxy," which means "milky" in Greek. Galaxies are named after their shapes, such as elliptical, spiral, or irregular galaxies. There are just a few galaxies other than ours that can be seen with the naked eye, yet scientists number the galaxies in our universe in the billions.

Science and Engineering Practices: Obtaining, Evaluating, and Communicating Information

Students can digitally thumb through the photo album of distant galaxies at the Hubble telescope website at hubblesite.org. Here, they can work in teams to select a galaxy to research and present to the class. Encourage students to think of different ways to classify and describe selected galaxies. Point out certain ones, such as the Sombrero Galaxy and the Tadpole Galaxy, to spark their interest.

EXPLORE
Mama Tia's Stars

Mama Tia loved a clean house. Everything had to be in its rightful place. That can be a very hard job—especially in Mama Tia's house. Mama Tia lived beyond the skies. Her home was far away with the sun, moon, and stars. Into her arms she would gather each newly formed star. Then, she would fling each bundle of stars high above her head. There, they would glow and twinkle as a new galaxy. She would reach up and spin each galaxy very gently. Off each galaxy would go, spinning through space. Each galaxy held millions of stars. And now there were so many galaxies! But still, she kept working, keeping her house in order.

The story of Mama Tia is a myth. A myth is a story about a natural event. But, like galaxies, these stories are stretched and stretched beyond the truth! Still, there are some facts in a myth. Can you find any in this story? With a partner, list facts you can find in the story of Mama Tia.

....

Ready? Take

DIG DEEPER
Beyond the Milky Way

To the early Romans, the tiny stars scattered across a twinkling band in the night sky resembled a starry road. This is how our galaxy, the Milky Way, came to be named. You and another astronomer have been studying this galaxy that rotates through space with its arms created by millions of stars. But your coworker thinks the name should be changed. This idea of a milky way is all in the past, he claims. He has a better, more accurate, name and a reason why this name should now be used. Present his case.

....

Ready? Take

NGSS

1-ESS1.A: The Universe and its Stars

5-ESS1.A: The Universe and its Stars

CCSS

W.K.2, W.1.2, W.2.2: Support with Facts

W.3.2, W.4.2, W.5.2: Clarity

ADDITIONAL RESOURCES

Discover the stars' place in the universe at http://www.discovery.com Search: "Big Stars"

Watch as a star is born at http://hubblesite.org/gallery/movie_theater/starslife/

Stars by Kristine Carlson Asselin. Capstone: 2011. (3–6)

Stars and Constellations by Nick Hunter. Heinemann-Raintree: 2013. (1–3)

LANGUAGE LINK		LEARNING SETTING
Explore:	Informative Writing	Individual
Dig Deeper:	Informative Writing	Individual

Stars

Science Information

As Earth travels around the sun, we look out at different areas of the Milky Way Galaxy. Year after year we see the same stars at the same time of year because Earth follows the same path each year. Many, many of these stars outclass our sun in both size and brightness, yet they seem as tiny points of light. The sun is so huge and bright because it is so close. The sun's light energy reaches us in about eight minutes. The next closest star, Proxima Centauri, looks like a faint dot, and its light takes more than four years to reach Earth. Light from Rigel, a star 20 times more massive than the sun and one of the brightest stars in the night sky, takes about 800 years to reach Earth.

Science and Engineering Practices: Planning and Carrying Out Investigations

Present students with a question: How does size and distance affect what we see? Then challenge them to develop investigations that support the claim that a larger object can appear smaller if it is farther away. Students might use flashlights of various sizes and brightnesses in a darkened room or balls of various sizes at different distances. How does this relate to our view of stars from Earth and their actual sizes?

Hot, Hotter, Hottest!

Look into the night sky. See the stars. They may all look white, but they are not. Stars can also be yellow, red, or blue. Think of a roaring fire. It may look like one big orange ball of fire, but it's not. Its flames are made of many colors—just like the stars. Red stars are the coolest stars. Orange stars are a little hotter. The next colors are yellow, white, and then blue. Blue stars are the hottest stars!

Draw a night sky on the black paper. Sprinkle these stars of different temperatures across the paper. Make 2 blue stars, 4 white stars, 5 yellow stars, and 4 orange stars. Place them in order from coolest to hottest. Below this night sky, answer this question: Can a star change colors? Why or why not?

....

Ready? Take

DIG DEEPER

A Star Is Born

Your science teacher distributed this handout. It describes the birth of a star. The teacher's handout reads:

"Far away in the universe a cloud of dust and gas becomes trapped into a contracting mass. It is getting smaller and smaller. This bundle gradually begins to heat up as it contracts even more, creating its own gravity. More dust and other particles get pulled into this mass. Finally, this mass gets heavier and heavier until it collapses under its own weight into a hot heap. A star is born."

Your friend doesn't quite understand it. He needs a little help. Explain the handout in your own unique way. Feel free to provide additional ideas of your own.

....

Ready? Take

Super Powers

Science
Notebook

*Trial of the
Century*

Science
Notebook

NGSS

1-ESS1.A: The
Universe and
its Stars

5-ESS1.A: The
Universe and
its Stars

CCSS

W.K.3, W.1.3,
W.2.3: Imagined
Experiences

W.3.1, W.4.1,
W.5.1: Claim
and Evidence

ADDITIONAL RESOURCES

NOVA provides a close-up view
of our largest star at The Sun
Lab at http://www.pbs.org/
wgbh/nova/labs/lab/sun/

Discover the "Secrets of the Sun"
at http://www.pbs.org/wgbh/
nova/space/secrets-sun.html

Sing along with songs about the sun
at http://www.watchknowlearn.
org Search: "Sun Songs"

The Sun by Nick Hunter.
Heinemann-Raintree: 2012. (3–6)

*Where Does the Sun Go At Night?
An Earth Science Mystery* by Amy
S. Hansen. Capstone: 2011. (1–2)

LANGUAGE LINK		LEARNING SETTING
Explore:	Narrative Writing	Individual
Dig Deeper:	Opinion	Individual

Sun

Science Information

Like all stars, the sun is a huge ball of gases. When atoms of
hydrogen at the star's core fuse into helium, energy that eventually
transforms into light moves outward from the sun's surface and
travels very quickly to Earth and beyond. Because light energy
travels in straight lines, we see the sun only when our side of Earth
faces it.

To ancient peoples, it was difficult to tell whether Earth moved
around the sun or vice versa. Not until the early 1500s did Nicolaus
Copernicus develop the heliocentric theory that described how
Earth and all of the heavenly bodies moved around the sun.
Another famous scientist, Galileo Galilei, later studied Copernicus's
ideas and believed them to be accurate. Yet it would take several
years after Galileo's death before the physics was developed that
would prove Copernicus's naked-eye observations correct.

Science and Engineering Practices: Using Mathematics and Computational Thinking

The sun contains 98.86 percent of the mass in our solar system. The
gas giants—Jupiter and Saturn—make up most of the remaining
1.14 percent of the solar system's mass. The four rocky inner planets,
which include Earth, have comparatively insignificant masses.
The sun has 333,000 times more mass than Earth, and the sun's
diameter is 109 times that of Earth. Help students to visualize scale
comparisons of this data. For example, 6'8" professional basketball
player Brittney Griner (sun diameter) could hold a penny (Earth
diameter). The average sized door frame compares to a nickel in the
same analogy.

EXPLORE
Super Powers

What is the center of our solar system? The sun!

What is the closest star to Earth? The sun!

What is the same size of a million planet Earths? The sun!

But that's not all! This super-sized star has even more power! What other questions could be answered with the response "The sun!"

Write at least two. And don't forget to write the answer!

....

Ready? Take

DIG DEEPER
Trial of the Century

Hundreds of years ago, people were amazed at the discoveries of Galileo and his "new and improved" telescope. Now, more planets and moons could be viewed and studied. Galileo's discoveries made history, but some people were not too happy with him. In fact, he had to go to court, where he was tried and punished. Why were they so upset? Galileo claimed Earth revolved around the sun. At the time, most people thought the sun revolved around Earth. "The sun is NOT the center of the universe," they argued. Suppose you are Galileo's attorney. Write your best argument to defend Galileo's theory. Be sure to make it a scientific-based argument with key scientific terms.

....

Ready? Take

LANGUAGE LINK		LEARNING SETTING
Explore:	Informative Writing	Individual
Dig Deeper:	Presentation	Individual

Moon Phases

Science Information

Earth's natural satellite—the moon—is about one-sixth Earth's size. It revolves around Earth in just over 27 days. During that time, its shape appears to change, going from a bright, full disk to nothing at all. These changing shapes, or phases, progress through a regular pattern based on the relative positions of Earth, the moon, and the sun. When we see the full moon, the moon is positioned on the opposite side of Earth from the sun. So we see the full effect of the sun's light reflecting off of the moon. We can't see the new moon because the moon is positioned between Earth and the sun. The sun's light is still reflecting off the moon's surface, but not in a direction that we can observe. The side of the moon facing Earth is unlighted. As the moon moves around Earth, we can see more and more of the lit side. We say that the moon is waxing, or growing. From full moon to new moon, when we can see less and less of the lighted side from Earth, we say that the moon is waning.

Science and Engineering Practices: Analyzing and Interpreting Data

Have students keep track of what time of day they can observe the moon over a month's period. Students should look for the moon at the same time each day, preferably in the early morning or late afternoon, no matter if it is light or dark out. Have them use their data to refute the claim that the moon is an object only seen in the nighttime sky.

It's Just a Phase

Can the moon change shapes? Of course not. It's just a trick of light. The sun's light hits the moon, and it bounces off. Sometimes we see all of the moon. Sometimes we see a small sliver. The other part of the moon is in darkness. But it is still there. Each month it goes through this same pattern of shapes, called "phases."

Draw a line across the middle of your paper. Use a black circle and trace four circles on the line. Glue one of the black circles on the first moon. Cut the other black circle in half. Glue the left half on the left side on the second moon. Leave the third moon blank. Glue the right half on the right side on the fourth moon. Write *New Moon* above the first circle, *First Quarter* above the second, *Full Moon* above the third circle, and *Last Quarter* above the fourth circle. Does the sun have phases like the moon? Why or why not? Write your answer at the bottom of the page.

Ready? Take

DIG DEEPER
Flipped Out

In one month, eight phases of the moon can be seen in the night sky. These phases are the New Moon (completely dark), Waxing Crescent (a small sliver of light on the right of the dark moon), First Quarter (half visible on the right), Waxing Gibbous (3/4ths visible on the right), Full Moon (completely illuminated), Waning Gibbous (sliver of darkness on the right), Last Quarter (left side illuminated), and the Waning Crescent (sliver of light on the left side). Draw and label each of the eight phases on the note cards. Place them in order and staple along the left side. Flip and view the phases of the moon. Next, use the blank side to describe this lunar event in eight words, one word per card. Now that's a challenge!

When you've finished, present your descriptions to classmates. Are your words the same—or not?

....

Night and Day

Science Information

The change from light to darkness is caused by the rotation of Earth. From our perspective, the sun appears to revolve around Earth, rising in the east and setting in the west. Wherever Earth faces the sun, light shines on that side of Earth. At the same time, the side facing away from the sun is experiencing night. As Earth continues to rotate on its axis, the places once in darkness will gradually turn to face the sun as a new day begins. Since Earth's axis is tilted, there is an uneven division of day and night. When the southern hemisphere is tilted toward the sun (summer), it has a longer day and shorter night than the northern hemisphere (winter). As Earth revolves, the northern hemisphere is tilted toward the sun and the day/night conditions reverse.

Science and Engineering Practices: Developing and Using Models

Use a beach ball and a flashlight to demonstrate the revolution of Earth around the sun. With the ball tilted slightly, move it around the flashlight (the sun). Observe where light strikes the ball. Use the observations to support claims about why some areas of Earth have longer daylight periods than other areas during different months.

PROMPT SUPPLIES

The Longest Day	*Watch This Show!*
Science Notebook	Science Notebook

NGSS	CCSS
1-ESS1.A: The Universe and its Stars	W.K.2, W.1.2, W.2.2: Support with Details
5-ESS1.B: Earth and the Solar System	W.3.1, W.4.1, W.5.1: Support with Reasons

ADDITIONAL RESOURCES

View an astronomer explaining the difference between day and night at http://museumvictoria.com.au/ Search: "day and night"

View the lights of Earth from space at http://www.sservi.nasa.gov/ Search: "Earth at night"

Day & Night by Teddy Newton. Chronicle Books: 2010. (K–3) The short film based on this story may also be found on the Internet from Pixar Animation.

Where Does the Sun Go at Night? An Earth Science Mystery by Amy S. Hansen. Capstone: 2011. (1–2)

The Longest Day

Up! Down! Go! Stop! Open! Close! What in the world? This is the world of opposites! What about night? The opposite of night is day! During the day, our side of Earth faces the sun. Slowly, this side of Earth turns away from the sun. What if our side of Earth always faced the sun? List or draw two ways life would be different.

Ready? Take

©2016 Kaye Hagler and Judy Elgin Jensen from *Take 5! for Science*. This page may be reproduced for classroom use only.

Watch This Show!

You are a television director, and you have been hired to direct a new science program. It is a documentary about night and day. It will explain how Earth rotates on its axis and revolves around the sun. You really want people to watch this show. Write a press release to send to all media outlets—television, newspapers, Internet. Include a catchy title and a description of this new program, one that will be sure to capture everyone's attention. Include at least two important reasons why viewers should watch this program. Be sure to use at least one science term related to the topic.

Ready? Take

©2016 Kaye Hagler and Judy Elgin Jensen from *Take 5! for Science*. This page may be reproduced for classroom use only.

LANGUAGE LINK		LEARNING SETTING
Explore:	Informative Writing	Individual
Dig Deeper:	Presentation	Collaboration

Shadows

Science Information

A shadow is a dark image of an object made when the object blocks light. Transparent, translucent, and opaque features of materials have to be considered when observing shadows. Transparent objects do not cast shadows. Translucent objects, like a red glass vase, would cast a lighter shaded shadow. Opaque objects block all of the light and cast distinct shadows that clearly represent the shapes of the objects. Opaque objects cast shadows that are very dark. The distance and angle of the light source in relation to the object that blocks the light changes the size and shape of the shadow that is cast. That's one way approximate time of day can be estimated from shadows.

Science and Engineering Practices: Constructing Explanations and Designing Solutions

Egyptians are credited for creating the first time device, a sundial, which measured time through the use of shadows. Medieval Europeans, the Chinese, and the Egyptians all created their own forms of a sundial. Encourage students to work in teams to research different types of sundials and create their own working timepieces from cardboard and rulers or dowels. Or create a simple sundial for younger students and help them analyze how it works.

PROMPT SUPPLIES

Shadow Machine	*Puppet Theater*
Science Notebook	Science Notebook

NGSS	CCSS
1-ESS1.A: The Universe and its Stars	W.K.2, W.1.2, W.2.2: Support with Facts
1-PS4.B: Electromagnetic Radiation	SL.3.4, SL.4.4, SL.5.4: Reports
5-ESS1.B: Earth and the Solar System	

ADDITIONAL RESOURCES

Change the size of shadows in this interactive experiment at http://www.sciencekids.co.nz/gamesactivities/lightshadows.html

Watch this fairy tale told through shadow puppets at https://www.tes.co.uk/teaching-resource/Teachers-TV-Making-Shadows-6085139

Shadows on My Wall by Timothy Young. Schiffer: 2012. (PreK–1)

We All Have Shadows by Maryellen Gregoire. Capstone: 2014. (PreK–1)

EXPLORE
Shadow Machine

It is so hot on the beach! The sun shines right on you. You need help. You need a shadow. A shadow acts like shade. It blocks the rays of the sun. You need a shadow, but you don't have an umbrella. Look around the beach. Use any natural objects. Draw a picture of you on the beach. Place yourself in the shadow of two different objects. Which one worked best? Why?

....

Ready? Take

DIG DEEPER
Puppet Theater

In a small group, create a brief skit using shadow puppets. Your team will develop a script that explains the role of the sun in creating shadows. Use a minimum of five lines of dialogue in your skit.

At a later time, you can rehearse and perform your skit for the class!

....

Ready? Take

Rotation/Revolution

Science Information

It's a surprise we don't get dizzy with Earth spinning around its axis at about 1,037 mph (1,670 kph) while it travels around the sun at about 66,673 mph (107,300 kph). Even at those speeds, it takes one day for Earth to complete one rotation and one year for it to complete one revolution. All planets rotate and revolve, and we commonly use the term "day" to define the rotation period and "year" to define the revolution period. On Jupiter, one year equals about 12 Earth years, but one day takes only about 10 Earth hours. The farther away a planet is from the sun, the longer its orbit, or path, around the sun.

Science and Engineering Practices: Using Mathematical and Computational Thinking

Work with students to create shapes that are elliptical (oval) and make relationships to the orbits of the planets as they revolve around the sun. Models are readily available on the Internet. While Earth's orbit is said to be elliptical, it is nearly circular. On the other hand, the orbit of Pluto (a dwarf planet) is so elliptical that it sometimes comes inside the orbit of Neptune, the farthest most planet.

PROMPT SUPPLIES

Take a Spin!	*Basketball Science*
Science Notebook	Science Notebook

NGSS	CCSS
1-ESS1.A: The Universe and its Stars	W.K.2, W.1.2, W.2.2: Support with Facts
5-ESS1.B: Earth and the Solar System	W.3.2.C, W.4.2.C, W.5.2.C: Transitions

ADDITIONAL RESOURCES

Students will enjoy the beat of this rapping video at https://www.flocabulary.com/solar-system/

Experience an astronaut's view of Earth in videos, such as https://www.youtube.com/results?search_query=breath+taking+time+lapse

Student demonstrations of rotation can be found at http://www.teachertube.com/ Search: "Rotation"

Max Goes to the Space Station: A Science Adventure with Max the Dog by Jeffrey Bennett and Michael Carroll. Big Kid Science: 2013. (2–4)

The Planets of Our Solar System by Steve Kortenkamp. Capstone: 2011. (3–4)

Take a Spin!

Let's rotate!

You are like Earth. You can go around and around. (All spin in place.)

Let's add the sun and make a revolution! (Move around a partner. Continue spinning.)

Now stop!

Is your head still spinning? Write and draw your answers to these questions.

1. Earth rotates. What is it doing?

2. Earth makes a revolution. What is it doing?

3. Name another object that rotates and explain why. Name another object that revolves and explain why.

....

Ready? Take

Basketball Science

Keegan loves to play basketball. Not only is he a star player, but he also can do tricks on the court with a basketball. One trick he likes to do is spin the ball on one finger. The force he applies sets the ball into a rotating motion as it balances on his finger. One day in science class, his teacher was describing Earth's rotation on its axis. A lightbulb suddenly went off in Keegan's head. "It's kind of like my basketball spin," he informed the class. Finish Keegan's comparison. How does he connect these two different items? Create two more comparisons to Earth's revolution around the sun.

"_____ is like Earth's revolution around the sun because _____."

Ready? Take

PROMPT SUPPLIES

The Four Seasons	*The Longest Summer*
Science Notebook	Science Notebook
Colored pencils	

NGSS

1-ESS1.B: Earth and the Solar System

5-ESS1.B: Earth and the Solar System

CCSS

W.K.1, W.1.1, W.2.1: Support with Reasons

W.3.1, W.4.1, W.5.1: Support with Reasons

ADDITIONAL RESOURCES

Why do seasons change? Find the answer at websites, such as http://www. neok12.com Search: "What causes the seasons?"

Computer animation explains the seasons at http://www. watchknowlearn.org Search: "Computer Animation of the Earth's Seasons"

A simple explanation of the four seasons can be found at turtlediary.com Search: "seasons"

Changing Seasons Acorn set by Rebecca Rissman and Sian Smith. Heinemann-Raintree: 2012. (Pre K–1)

Exploring the Seasons, a four-set series, by Terri DeGezelle. Capstone: 2012. (K–2)

LANGUAGE LINK		LEARNING SETTING
Explore:	Opinion	Individual
Dig Deeper:	Opinion	Individual

Seasons

Science Information

Earth has four seasons: spring, summer, fall, and winter. Each season is a pattern of temperature changes and weather trends that change over the course of a year. The four seasons result from the tilt of Earth's axis. Because Earth's axis is tilted, different parts of the planet receive different amounts of solar energy during Earth's revolution around the sun. The hemisphere tilted toward the sun receives more solar energy and experiences the warmer seasons of spring and summer. The hemisphere tilted away from the sun receives less solar energy and experiences the cooler seasons of fall and winter.

Science and Engineering Practices: Developing and Using Models

Students can make a folding graphic organizer with a pane for each of the seasons. After labeling each pane with the name of a season, students might create a diagram in each pane that depicts and explains how Earth's seasons are caused by the changing positions of Earth and the sun. Younger students might simply draw appropriate clothing for each season.

EXPLORE
The Four Seasons

Genny loves to read. Her favorite spot is a window seat in her family's home in Tennessee. Here, she can watch the hills turn to orange in the fall. In the winter, the bare limbs catch the snow. In spring, the first shoots in her mother's flower beds appear. By summer, the hills are green again. Her friend Katherine lives in Hawaii. Here, there are only two seasons: summer and winter. But the winter is also warm. In Hawaii, summers are dry, and winters are wet. Would you prefer to have four seasons or only two? Support your opinion with at least two reasons.

Ready? Take

DIG DEEPER
The Longest Summer

Weather patterns change during Earth's yearlong trek around the sun. When Earth's North Pole tilts toward the sun, summer conditions can be felt in the northern hemisphere. When it tilts away from the sun, the northern hemisphere experiences winter conditions. Earth's axis tilts at 23.5 degrees. Like Earth, Mars also tilts on its axis, at approximately 25 degrees. It also has seasons—with several major differences. The most important difference is the length of seasons on Mars. We think of summer as June, July, and August. On Mars, seasons can last up to seven months. Would you like for our seasons to be as long as those on Mars? Why or why not? Give reasons to support your answers.

Ready? Take

Endangered Species
Change
Invertebrates
Fossils
Plants
Ecosystem
The Senses
Migration
Extinction
Seeds
Populations
Behavior
Consumers
Food Chain
Habitat
Photosynthesis
Heredity
Adaptation
Biodiversity
Producers
Biomes
Decomposers Hibernation Vertebrates

Chapter 3:
Life Science Prompts

PROMPT SUPPLIES

Polar Bear Biome

Science Notebook

Colored pencils

Swamp Creatures

Science Notebook

NGSS

2-LS4.D: Biodiversity and Humans

3-LS4.D: Biodiversity and Humans

CCSS

W.K.2, W.1.2, W.2.2: Support with Facts

W.3.2, W.4.2, W.5.2: Support with Facts

ADDITIONAL RESOURCES

Introduce a lesson on biomes with videos, such as this one found at http://ed.ted.com/on/b7hfcQqs

Discover a wide range of photos and information on the world's major biomes at http://earthobservatory. nasa.gov/Experiments/Biome/

Many Biomes, One Earth by Sneed B. Collard III. Charlesbridge Press: 2009. (1–3)

LANGUAGE LINK		LEARNING SETTING
Explore:	Informative Writing	Individual
Dig Deeper:	Informative Writing	Individual

Biomes

Science Information

Earth can be divided into regions by climate and the mix of organisms that are found in them. Generally, Earth is divided into five biomes. Tundra biomes are treeless arctic areas that are permanently frozen below the ground's surface. Deserts are barren areas that can be warm (Sahara) or cold (Antarctic). They usually receive 10 or fewer inches of rain per year. Forests that are crucial for many diverse life forms cover one-third of Earth. Taiga forests dominated by conifers are found in locations with short summers. Biomes with shorter winters have temperate deciduous forests—trees that lose their leaves in winter. Rain forests are found in the tropics and are the richest biome in terms of biodiversity. Grasslands include three main forms: savannas (with scattered trees), temperate (almost no trees), and steppes (found in interiors of Europe and North America). Because almost three-fourths of Earth is covered by water, the aquatic biome is the largest. It includes all of the things that live around, on, or in the water.

Science and Engineering Practices: Asking Questions and Defining Problems

Have teams of students brainstorm a list of questions they have about biomes and how they would investigate the answer to one of their questions. For example, to answer a question like "How is temperature related to the kinds of plants in an area?" students might explore the regions or latitudes where the various biomes generally occur on Earth.

EXPLORE

Polar Bear Biome

Camels live in the desert. It is hot and dry there. Monkeys and parrots live in a rain forest. It is very wet and warm there. A rain forest and a desert are two biomes. A biome is a large, natural area. It is home to special plants and animals. It can be hot, cold, or warm. It can be very wet or dry. But what about a polar bear? Could it live in a desert? Could it live in a rain forest?

Draw a polar bear in its biome. Now finish this sentence: "A polar bear's biome needs to be _____."

Draw a whale in its biome. Now finish this sentence: "A whale's biome needs to be _____."

....

Ready? Take 5!

DIG DEEPER

Swamp Creatures

The entire Okefenokee Wildlife Refuge, located in the southeastern United States, covers almost 400,000 acres! It is one of the largest freshwater ecosystems in the entire world. Okefenokee's large ecosystem is in a deciduous forest biome. Other deciduous forest biomes can be found in China and Japan. The deciduous forest biomes enjoy four seasons, have a temperature range of 30–70°F (-1–21°C), and have average rainfall of 32 inches (81 centimeters). Think of at least two plants and animals that could NOT live in this biome. Why could they not live there? Include the words "ecosystem" and "biome" in your answer.

....

Ready? Take 5!

NGSS

2-LS4.D: Biodiversity and Humans

5-LS2.A: Interdependent Relationships in Ecosystems

CCSS

W.K.1, W.1.1, W.2.1: Support with Facts

W.3.1, W.4.1, W.5.1: Support with Facts

ADDITIONAL RESOURCES

National Geographic provides an assortment of coloring pages of different ecosystems online at http://education.nationalgeographic.com/education/coloring-page/?ar_a=1

Watch the opening 2:30 minutes of "Open Ocean Ecosystems Explained," taken from Finding Nem at http://www.dnatube.com/video/7297/Open-Ocean-Ecosystems-explained

Ecosystems by Jenny Fretland VanVoorst. Abdo: 2014. (3–5)

Exploring Ecosystems with Max Axiom, Super Scientist by Agnieszka Biskup. Capstone: 2007. (3–6)

LANGUAGE LINK		LEARNING SETTING
Explore:	Informative Writing	Pair
Dig Deeper:	Informative Writing	Individual

Ecosystem

Science Information

Ecosystems are made up of more than just the living things in an area—they also include the nonliving parts, such as air, water, and soil. Ecosystems can range in size from the very large, such as the Mojave Desert, to the very small, such as the upturned water-catching leaves of a bromeliad. One bromeliad's watery ecosystem can be home to an assortment of living things, including insects, frogs, spiders, and earthworms. Even this tiny ecosystem displays a delicate balance. Introducing a foreign organism, such as a nonnative insect or slug, might destroy the ecosystem because the nonnative animal likely would have no natural predators

Science and Engineering Practices: Planning and Carrying Out Investigations

Have students draw a picture of an ecosystem. On the reverse side, have them draw a tool they could use to learn more about the ecosystem they have chosen. They should be able to explain why the tool will be useful. Students might use tools, such as thermometers (to compare temperatures in different areas), meter sticks (to measure population density), hand lenses (to see small organisms), netting (to capture flying organisms), and so on. Have students add a caption that explains why they are using the tools they suggest.

EXPLORE

Home Sweet Home

Look carefully at the picture. This seagull is at home in its ecosystem. An ecosystem is more than plants and animals. It is also the air, water, and soil in an area. What can be found in a seagull's ecosystem? With a partner, make a list. Name two things you see in its ecosystem. Then, name two things that would not be found in a seagull's ecosystem. Why wouldn't you find these items there?

....

 **Ready? Take**

Goldfish Invasion

Flathead Lake in Montana is called one of the cleanest lakes in America. The water is so clear, you can see as far down as 20 feet (about 6 meters) into the water. As a local fish and wildlife ranger, you enjoy your job. It is exciting to inform visitors to Flathead Lake about the many plant and animal habitats that coexist here. This ecosystem is their home. Wait a minute! What is that kid doing? He has a plastic bag filled with water and . . . a goldfish!

"Don't put that into the lake!" you call.

The boy looks up. "Why not? It's just a fish."

Just a fish? Here, it is against the law to release goldfish into the wild. That was a close one, but you intercepted this unwanted visitor before it hit the lake. Now it's time to answer his question. As the wildlife ranger, you know the dangers of discarding aquarium fish and plants or even nonnative bait like earthworms into an established ecosystem. What do you tell the young visitor to the park? You need to be firm, yet gentle.

Ready? Take

Biodiversity

Science Information

The greater the number of species in a given ecosystem (no matter how large or small), the more likely the ecosystem itself will thrive. If something happens to change the environment and one species dies out, there will be others to fill in the food chains and other roles. In 1980, Thomas Lovejoy was the first to use the term "biological diversity," since shortened to "biodiversity," and he has dedicated his life to preserving it. This idea of the importance of the variety of life around the globe includes both variety in the genes within a species and the number of different species. A species with a lot of variations in their genes will more likely adapt to changes in the environment.

Science and Engineering Practices: Obtaining, Evaluating, and Communicating Information

Share with students that the United Nations declared that the period 2011–2020 is "the United Nations Decade on Biodiversity." Students might research the role of zoos in this effort. One example is the National Zoo, which has worked to help giant pandas, tigers, and black-footed ferrets, among others, to recover. Along with research, zoos create awareness of issues. Students might virtually visit the giant panda enclosure at the National Zoo to read and make observations. Guide them to summarize their findings as statements supported facts.

PROMPT SUPPLIES

Something Different	*Go Wild*
Science Notebook	Science Notebook

NGSS	CCSS
2-LS4.D: Biodiversity and Humans	L.K.5.A, L.1.5.A, L.2.5.A: Sorting
3-LS4.D: Biodiversity and Humans	W.3.2.B, W.4.2.B, W.5.2.B: Develop Topic with Facts and Details

ADDITIONAL RESOURCES

Watch as scientists measure biodiversity in a rainforest at http://www.nhm.ac.uk/discover/borneo-biodiversity-count.html

Student filmmakers have tackled biodiversity with informative videos, such as those found at http://www.savingspecies.org/2011/top-35-biodiversity-videos/

A variety of activities for teachers on biodiversity can be found at http://www.environment.nsw.gov.au/resources/education/biodiversityteachersguide.pdf

Students can view the biodiversity found in a rain forest in http://www.pbskids.org/dragonflytv/show/biodiversity.html

Tree of Life: The Incredible Biodiversity of Life on Earth by Rochelle Strauss. Kids Can Press: 2013. (3–7)

Something Different

Our world is made of many different, or diverse, plants and animals. "Bio" means "life." Therefore, "bio" (life) + "diversity" (different) = biodiversity, or different kinds of life. Our world is a world of biodiversity. Imagine if there were only one kind of tree, flower, or animal. How boring! Write these topics on your paper: Pets, Bugs, Trees. With a partner, draw or list as many different examples of each topic in two minutes. Write the examples below the three topics. You will have three columns of biodiversity! Then, count the total number of examples. Write this on your paper. Share with your partner your favorite pet, bug, and tree. Explain why each is your favorite.

Ready? Take

DIG DEEPER

Go Wild

Healthy ecosystems can support a wide variety of living organisms. This is called "biodiversity." Take a hike through a forest. Here, biodiversity abounds with many different insects, birds, and other animals. Deer dart through a stand of trees, stopping occasionally to eat acorns and grass along their way. A sunning turtle feeds on small insects and plants in a small pond. Robins build their nest with feathers, moss, and twigs while feeding on grasshoppers, caterpillars, and blueberries.

According to the World Wildlife Fund, "The effects of human activities on biodiversity have increased so greatly that the rate of species extinctions is rising to hundreds or thousands of times." With a group, answer these questions:

What types of "human activities" affect a healthy biodiversity?

What could we do to help promote or protect biodiversity?

Ready? Take

Habitat

Science Information

The word "habitat" is often used interchangeably, though incorrectly, with terms, such as "ecosystem," "environment," and "biosphere." An organism's habitat is specific to the species itself and refers to the area where it lives within an ecosystem. The terms "ecosystem" and "biosphere," however, are much broader terms. An ecosystem contains many specific habitats—as many as there are different species of organisms in the ecosystem. An organism's habitat includes the living and nonliving factors needed for that organism to survive.

Science and Engineering Practices: Constructing Explanation and Designing Solutions

Have teams of students select a habitat and describe the ecosystem in which the habitat exists. Remind them that a habitat is specific to the plant, animal, or other organism that lives there, and many habitats exist in an ecosystem. Teams should explain how the habitat can exist in that particular locale and what the species gets from it that allows it to survive. For example, fleas can live in a dog's fur because that habitat provides a source of warmth and food. The dog itself lives in a different habitat in a much larger ecosystem.

PROMPT SUPPLIES

At the Zoo	*Hanging Out with Giraffes*
Science Notebook	Science Notebook

NGSS	CCSS
2-LS4.D: Biodiversity and Humans	SL.K.5, SL.1.5, SL.2.5: Description
3-LS4.D: Biodiversity and Humans	W.3.2.C, W.4.2.C, W.5.2.C: Transitions

ADDITIONAL RESOURCES

Take interactive journeys through different habitats at http://pbskids.org/wildkratts/habitats/

Examine photographs of different habitats at http://environment.nationalgeographic.com/environment/habitats/

Younger students will enjoy the interactive "Match the Habitat" game at http://www.cserc.org/main/games/matchthehabitat/index.html

Habitat Survival, a series of 8 books exploring different habitats, by Buffy Silverman, Claire Llewellyn, Melanie Waldron. Heinemann-Raintree: 2012. (2–4)

Nature's Patchwork Quilt: Understanding Habitats by Mary Miche. Dawn: 2012. (2–5)

At the Zoo

LaShaye was so excited. Her class was going to the zoo. There, she saw all kinds of animals. Her favorite was the giraffe! She had so many questions for her teacher.

"Are they safe in their pen? Where do they get food?"

"The zookeepers take care of the animals. They have made a special place for giraffes," the teacher explained.

"Is this like their home?" LaShaye asked again.

The teacher explained. "This is like their habitat in the grasslands of Africa."

Think of two other animals on view in a zoo. Describe a safe and comfortable habitat for these two animals. Include drawings for supporting details. Share your description and drawings with classmates.

....

Ready? Take

©2016 Kaye Hagler and Judy Elgin Jensen from *Take 5! for Science*. This page may be reproduced for classroom use only.

Hanging Out with Giraffes

Shhh! Don't move. Keep your binoculars handy. A herd of giraffes is moving through the tall grass coming this way. They are going toward that acacia tree, a common sight here in Africa. Watch and you will see them arch their long necks up into the tops of these trees to munch on leaves. The branches may be too thorny for other predators, but not for giraffes. They grab hold of the branches and rip the leaves away. An adult male can eat up to 145 pounds (66 kilograms) of leaves a day! Giraffes enjoy open grasslands, called "savannas," and warm to hot temperatures. This is their habitat, a place where all their needs for survival are met. Changes in a habitat can threaten the plants and animals that live there. Describe two changes that could threaten the habitat of the giraffe. Use linking words, such as "because" and "then."

Ready? Take

NGSS

K-ESS3.A: Natural Resources

3-LS4.D: Biodiversity and Humans

CCSS

W.K.2, W.1.2, W.2.2: Support with Facts

W.3.1.B, W.4.1.B, W.5.1.B: Support with Reasons

ADDITIONAL RESOURCES

Learn more about population dynamics at websites, such as http://video.nhptv.org/video/1491196512/

This short video provides important statistics of the decreasing populations of animals: https://www.youtube.com/watch?v=TPP6F5p33pg

Animals that Live in Groups by Kelsi Turner Tjernagel. Capstone: 2012. (1–2)

Earth's Growing Population by Catherine Chambers. Heinemann-Raintree: 2009. (3–5)

Understanding Animal Graphs (Real World Math-Level 3) by Dawn McMillan. Capstone: 2010. (2–3)

LANGUAGE LINK		LEARNING SETTING
Explore:	Informative Writing	Individual
Dig Deeper:	Opinion	Collaboration

Populations

Science Information

A population is a group of organisms of the same species that lives together in the same area. Each population has special needs that it obtains from the habitat in which it lives. Should conditions in the habitat change, the population will have to move to another habitat that can meet its needs. Populations within a given habitat often compete for limited resources. If resources become limited and the population is unable to relocate, the numbers of individuals in the population will decrease. Likewise, if habitat resources increase, population numbers will increase.

Science and Engineering Practices: Using Mathematics and Computational Thinking

Share the following data with students from a study conducted at Valley Forge National Historical Park on the white-tailed deer population there and in the surrounding countryside. Challenge students to analyze the data and suggest reasons why the survival rates vary inside and outside the park. Elicit why the survival rates for males and females outside the park are different from each other. Stimulate ideas by discussing the physical features of males and females and how they differ.

WHITE-TAILED DEER POPULATION	INSIDE THE PARK	OUTSIDE THE PARK	
Number out of every 100 deer	All deer	Males	Female
Deer that survive	83	27	60
Deer that die	17	73	40

You might decide to create similar data for a population students might see every day. For example, describe a feral cat population as one living totally outdoors finding food on its own. Compare them with a number of cats living with owners in an apartment building. Elicit from students why the size of the feral cat population might be smaller (or larger) than the pet cat population. Factors affecting population size include food availability, shelter, health care, quality of food, cars, age of the cats, and so on.

EXPLORE
Population Explosion

A herd of deer lives in a forest. In this forest, the herd has plenty of food, water, and shelter. It can survive here. The forest is also home to many different populations, or groups, of plants and animals. Oh no! Look! Here comes another herd of deer running this way. Their home has disappeared. Large bulldozers cut down all the trees in their habitat. But this forest isn't big enough for another herd of deer. The population of deer in the forest is exploding! Why is this a problem? You may include a drawing with your answer.

....

Ready? Take

DIG DEEPER
Oh, Deer!

The white-tailed deer population in St. Andrews State Park has gotten out of control. Native vegetation is quickly disappearing; new growth in trees has seriously decreased. The deer are upsetting the natural balance of other plants and animals in this ecosystem. What can be done? You are a member of the board of directors. The following options have been presented to the board:
- Fence sensitive plant populations
- Fence the entire park
- Introduce natural predators, such as wolves and coyotes
- Allow public hunting
- Capture many of the females and relocate them

Consult with the other members of the board. What is the best plan? Defend the board's decision with three reasons.

....

Ready? Take

Producers

Science Information

Producers do not get the energy for life processes from other organisms but make their own food through the process of photosynthesis. Plants, and other producers, such as algae, phytoplankton, and some types of bacteria, are able to use energy from sunlight and transform it into chemical energy that is stored in carbon compounds. They do this by combining water from soil or air and carbon dioxide from the air. Producers are at the first level of all food chains and the base of all food webs and energy pyramids. Everything beyond producers in a food chain eats producers or eats organisms that eat producers.

Science and Engineering Practices: Using Mathematics and Computational Thinking

Students might examine several energy pyramids to help determine the relative number of producers compared to the consumers in an ecosystem. Have them make claims about how energy pyramids, food webs, and food chains are alike and different. Claims should be backed by evidence. For example, the wider base of the energy pyramid reflects greater numbers of individuals and food webs and food chains tend to show only representative producers. Students should also notice that all three representations show the same energy flow from producers to various kinds of consumers.

PROMPT SUPPLIES

Let's Go Shopping	*Eat a "Light" Breakfast*
Science Notebook	Science Notebook
Colored pencils	Colored pencils

NGSS

K-LS1.C: Organization for Matter

5-PS2.D: Energy in Chemical Processes and Everyday Life

CCSS

L.K.5.A, L.1.5.A, L.2.5.A: Sorting

W.3.2, W.4.2, W.5.2: Support with Reasons

ADDITIONAL RESOURCES

Visit a farmers' market to explore the different fruits and vegetables available each season at http://www.nutrition.gov/farmers-markets

Do a search for "plants and energy" on the Internet. You might look at such sites as http://video.nhptv.org/video/1491187653/ Search: "Guide to plants"

Ocean Food Chains by Angela Royston. Heinemann-Raintree: 2014. (1–3)

Producing Vegetables by Casey Rand. Heinemann-Raintree: 2012. (4–6)

Let's Go Shopping

It's time to go to the grocery store. Let's get a shopping cart and head to the produce section. Here, we will find fruits and vegetables. How about some carrots and potatoes? Next, we need a bag of oranges. These fruits and vegetables are called "produce." Produce grows in gardens, fields, or orchards. All plants are producers. Why? Because they grow, or produce, their own food. How? They use light energy from the sun. Draw your shopping cart. Add five produce items to your grocery cart. Under the drawing, list the five producers in the cart. Rank them in order from number 1, your most favorite, to number 5, your least favorite. (Example: 1—blueberries!)

Ready? Take

DIG DEEPER

Eat a "Light" Breakfast

It is the day before the big race. You have been training for this event for six months. Each day you run the track at school, and you work out with weights in the gym. Most importantly, you eat energy foods. Plants are packed with energy. They use light energy from the sun to make their own food. This process is called "photosynthesis." "Synthesis" means "to come together." Light, air, and water all "come together" in a plant, so it can make its own food. We can't produce our own food, but we can eat producers. Producers supply important nutrients. Here are a few examples:

Vitamin A: dark, leafy vegetables; carrots; yellow fruits

Vitamin C: tomatoes, oranges, berries

Vitamin B1 and fiber: whole grains like whole wheat bread, oatmeal

Protein: peanut butter, nuts, dried beans, corn

Potassium: bananas, raisins, melons

Plan a producer meal. You must have four items on your plate. Draw the plate, and divide it into four sections. In each section draw the food item. Below the plate, explain the need to include producers in our diet. Then, explain what could happen if we do not include producers in our daily meals.

Ready? Take

PROMPT SUPPLIES

Frog Stew

Science
Notebook

Eat Your Words

Science
Notebook

NGSS

K-LS1.C:
Organization
for Matter and
Energy Flow in
Organisms

5-PS2.D: Energy
in Chemical
Processes and
Everyday Life

CCSS

W.K.1, W.1.1,
W.2.1: Claim
with Evidence

L.K.5.A, L.1.5.A,
L.2.5.A: Sorting

L.3.4.B, L.4.4.B,
L.5.4.B: Affixes
and Root Words

ADDITIONAL RESOURCES

Young students will enjoy this
interactive sorting activity at
http://switchzoo.com/games/
pleasedofeedtheanimals.htm

What's for lunch? Search with
students for websites about food
chains, such as http://education.
nationalgeographic.com/education/
encyclopedia/food-web/?ar_a=1

Food Chains and Webs, a six-
book set, by Angela Royston:
Capstone: 2015. (1–3)

LANGUAGE LINK		LEARNING SETTING
Explore:	Vocabulary/Opinion	Individual
Dig Deeper:	Vocabulary	Individual

Consumers

Science Information

What consumes what? is the question. Consumers are organisms
that cannot make their own food. Herbivores—consumers such
as birds, rabbits, zebras, and cows—eat only plants (producers).
Herbivores are called primary consumers because they eat the
producers directly. Omnivores are consumers that eat both other
animals and plants. Raccoons, grizzly bears, seagulls, and chickens
are omnivores. Carnivores are consumers that eat only other
animals. Hyenas, wolves, badgers, and cougars are carnivores.

Science and Engineering Practices: Developing and Using Models

Explain to students that the shape of an animal's teeth is a clue
to whether it is an herbivore, omnivore, or carnivore. Challenge
students to make models of teeth that they think might be
characteristic of each group. They might use clay or florist foam
or make simple drawings. Then work with students to find
photographs of real animal teeth of animals from each group.
Guide students to evaluate how their models are alike and
different from the real thing.

Frog Stew

The words "consume" and "eat" are verbs. They show action. You can eat food. You can also consume food. "Eat" and "consume" share the same meaning. Some animals consume meat. They are called "carnivores." A bird like the blue heron is a carnivore. It eats fish and frogs. Some animals consume plants. They are herbivores. A zebra eats twigs, leaves, and tree bark. It's an herbivore! Some animals consume both. They are omnivores. A monkey eats seeds, fruit, and insects. What about you? Are you a carnivore, herbivore, or omnivore? Support your answer with examples of foods you like to consume.

....

Ready? Take

Eat Your Words

Some animals eat only meat; they are carnivores. Some animals eat only plants; they are herbivores. Some eat both; they are called omnivores. Let's break these words down:

"Vore": a suffix that means "one who eats"

"Carne": French for "meat"

"Omni": Latin for "all"

"Herba": Latin for "grass" or "green crops"

Let's create new words using "vore" as the suffix. How about "dairyvore"—one who eats dairy products like ice cream or yogurt? Create three new words and provide their meanings.

....

Ready? Take

NGSS

K-LS1.C: Organization for Matter and Energy Flow in Organisms

5-LS2.A: Interdependent Relationships in Ecosystems

CCSS

W.K.2, W.1.2, W.2.1: Support with Facts

W.3.2.C, W.4.2.C, W.5.2.C: Transitions

ADDITIONAL RESOURCES

Discover "Decomposers and Scavengers" on the Internet in a video, such as http://video.nhptv.org/video/1491195223/

Time-lapse video features decomposers at work at pbslearningmedia.org Search: "Decomposers"

Decomposers [With Web Access] by Megan Lappi. Weigl Pub Inc.: 2011. (3–5)

LANGUAGE LINK		LEARNING SETTING
Explore:	Informative Writing	Individual
Dig Deeper:	Cause and Effect	Individual

Decomposers

Science Information

Plants are the producers that capture the energy of the sun and change it to chemical energy. This energy travels up the food chain as consumers eat plants and are eaten in turn. What about plants that aren't eaten or organisms that die without being eaten? Dead plants and animals contain energy that nature doesn't waste. A decomposer is an organism that eats dead matter, making use of the available energy, and recycling anything it doesn't consume back to the environment. Slugs, snails, flies, mites, bacteria, and fungi are all examples of decomposers.

Science and Engineering Practices: Asking Questions and Defining Problems

Guide students to understand that decomposers in natural environments work in the same way as those that break down, or rot, the food they eat. Encourage students to ask questions about decomposers that could be investigated. Students might pose questions related to the effect of cold temperatures, the presence of moisture, the influence of other kinds of foods nearby, and so on.

EXPLORE
The Food Chain Train

1

Choo, choo, choo, choo

Decomposers get on board

All worms, snails, and slugs.

2

There's one last stop

on this chain

A job made just for you.

3

Chew, chew, chew, chew

Break down leaves.

Break down bugs.

In each place, toss out your waste.

4

This feeds the soil

Renews the earth

And now the chain begins again.

Choo, choo, choo, choo

Words and music composed by Slug E

This song is about decomposers. Without decomposers, what happens to soil? Include the words "chain," "decomposers," and "because" in your answer. At a later time, recite this song with creative motions!

....

Ready? Take

Going Fishing

Terrell is going fishing with his grandfather. First, they get their fishing poles ready; then Terrell follows his grandfather to the garden. He watches as his grandfather digs in the dirt.

"What are you doing, Grandpa?" Terrell asks.

His grandfather pulls up two fat, wiggly worms.

"Grandpa," Terrell exclaims, "your garden is being invaded!"

His grandpa laughed. "Don't be silly! The more worms eat, the better the soil."

What is the connection between worms and rich soil? Use transitions, such as "because," "since," and "also" in your explanation.

....

Ready? Take

Food Chain

Science Information

The movement of energy from the sun through an ecosystem can be modeled in a food chain. That chain shows the transfer of light energy from the sun to plants and then to an animal that eats plants. The chain continues as long as one animal is eating another animal. At some point, an animal feeds and then dies without another animal eating it. Then the decomposers step in.

How does the energy move? The light energy changes into chemical energy in the plants. While the plant itself uses some of the energy, some is passed along to the plant-eating animals. Another animal eats the first animal. The chemical energy in the first one fuels the second. An animal that eats another animal is called a predator. Predators can be bigger, such as eagles and raccoons, or predators can be smaller, such as snakes and lizards.

Science and Engineering Practices: Engaging in Argument from Evidence

Have students select an organism (native or exotic) and gather information from research to develop a food chain. They can share evidence to prove that their food chains would be viable in nature. A keyword search, such as "grassland food chain" will give you examples to share with younger students. Then students could make statements about what they observe based on evidence that they can cite.

PROMPT SUPPLIES

Great Gulps of Energy	*Busted!*
Science Notebook	Science Notebook

NGSS

2-LS2.A: Interdependent Relationships in Ecosystems

5-LS2.A: Interdependent Relationships in Ecosystems

CCSS

W.K.3, W.1.3, W.2.3: Sequence

W.3.3, W.4.3, W.5.3: Sequence

ADDITIONAL RESOURCES

The Florida Everglades is the setting for the video on the food chain at http://www.odysseyearth.com/videos/the-food-chain/

Take a dramatic journey alongside tiny marine creatures, important links in the ocean's food chain, at http//www.nationalgeographic.com/ Search: "Krill"

Food Chains and Webs, a six-book set, by Angela Royston. Heinemann-Raintree: 2015. (1–3)

The World of Food Chains with Max Axion, Super Scientist by Liam O'Donnell. Capstone: 2007. (3–4)

EXPLORE

Great Gulps of Energy

The garden snail is slow and hungry. It sees a leaf in its path. It crawls toward its lunch. Gulp! The snail now has some of the leaf's energy. Uh-oh! It's still much too slow. A frog now sees the snail. The frog is also hungry. Gulp! The frog has some of the snail's energy now. It hops back to his home in the pond. Uh-oh! Here comes a large bird. It is also very hungry. Gulp! It now has some of the energy of the leaf, the snail, the frog. What is hungry next? Maybe a snake, a fish, or a large bird? Draw each step in this food chain. Begin with the leaf and then the snail. Connect each object with arrows to show the next step in the food chain. See how far you can take this food chain. Under the drawing complete this sentence: "A food chain helps _____."

Ready? Take

DIG DEEPER

Busted!

It seemed like a good plan at the time. Carson just wanted to get rid of a pesky wasp that buzzed around him as he played basketball. He read that wasps are attracted to sweets, so he dropped some honey into a small plastic bottle. He then placed the bottle on the ground beneath the net and turned on a remote camera. Boy, did he get a surprise the next morning! There was no sign of the wasp—or the bottle. Here is what he saw.

First, the wasp became stuck in the honey, causing the bottle to tip over. A large, hungry beetle heard the noise and quickly scurried in and devoured the wasp. A lizard passing by saw the beetle, stuck its head in the bottle for a quick lunch, but then became stuck. And so it goes in the events of this food chain. Now, it's your turn. Where did the bottle go? You and a partner will complete this simple narrative with two to three additional predators. Be sure to use transitions to link the sequence of events.

Ready? Take 5!

LANGUAGE LINK		LEARNING SETTING
Explore:	Informative Writing	Individual
Dig Deeper:	Language	Individual

Plants

Science Information

Without plants, life as we know it wouldn't exist because we, as consumers, cannot use the sun's energy directly. Luckily, plants are prolific! Evidence is in the number of seeds in the foods we eat—a tomato or sweet pepper can be chock full of them. Each sweet pepper seed, in the right environment, can grow into a sweet pepper plant that can produce more peppers with even more seeds. Not all plants produce seeds, but all do reproduce more of their own kind, and usually a lot of them. The general types of plants are mosses and liverworts, horsetails, ferns, conifers, and flowering plants. Some classification schemes also include green algae with plants.

Science and Engineering Practices: Obtaining, Evaluating, and Communicating Information

Point out to students that flowering plants make up about 90 percent of the 250,000 or more species of plants on Earth, and that they are a very diverse lot. Explain that flowers are the way these plants reproduce and that flowers are where seeds form. You might challenge students to find "extremes" in flower size and structure and seed size and shape. Show younger students pictures of some of those extremes, such as tiny duckweed, huge rafflesia, smelly corpse flower, coconuts, poppy seeds, and so on. An Internet search of "bizarre" or "unusual flowers" or "sizes of seeds" will yield many examples.

PROMPT SUPPLIES

Book Worm

5 blank note cards cut in half (or sheets of card stock cut in fourths)

Colored pencils

Rewriting Mother Goose

Science Notebook

NGSS

2-LS3.A: Inheritance of Traits

3-LS1.B: Growth and Development of Organisms

CCSS

W.K.2, W.1.2, W.2.2: Support with Facts

L.3.3.A, L.4.3.A, L.5.3.A: Word Choice

ADDITIONAL RESOURCES

Watch as time-lapse video reveals the transition from a seed to a flower at pbslearningmedia.org/ Search: "From seed to flower"

It takes patience to grow a flower as Peep soon learns in http:// peepandthebigwideworld.com/en/ kids/videos/35/peep-plants-a-seed/

Isabella's Garden by Glenda Millard. Candlewick Press: 2012. (K–2)

Plants by Melanie Waldron. Heinemann-Raintree: 2014. (4–6)

Book Worm

Create your own mini book. Place the 9 cards on top of each other. This book is about how plants grow. Draw only on the front of each card. On the front write a title. At the bottom of each page leave a space for writing. Number the pages on the top right.

On page 1, draw a mound of dirt.

On page 2, add a seed to the dirt.

On page 3, cover the seed with more dirt.

On page 4, draw the same picture as 3 but add rain.

On page 5, do the same as 4 but add the sun on the top left.

On page 6, draw a small shoot with no leaves. Move the sun slightly.

On page 7, draw a bigger plant with one leaf. Move the sun.

On page 8, draw the plant even bigger. Move the sun slightly.

On page 9, write and complete this sentence: "Plants need_____, _____, and _____ to grow." Add many plants and a bright sun! The End.

Staple the pages along the left side. Flip through the book quickly from front to back. Watch the plant grow!

DIG DEEPER
Rewriting Mother Goose

A popular Mother Goose rhyme goes like this:

> "Mary, Mary, quite contrary
>
> How does your garden grow?
>
> With silver bells and cockle shells
>
> And pretty maids all in a row."

Wait a minute! That's not right! The science is all wrong—it takes good soil, sunshine, air, and water to grow a garden. Rewrite the last two lines of this poem, keeping the same rhyme scheme.

Ready? Take

LANGUAGE LINK		LEARNING SETTING
Explore:	Narrative Writing	Individual
Dig Deeper:	Opinion	Pair

Photosynthesis
Science Information

The process of photosynthesis is our connection to the sun's energy and the reason life on Earth thrives. Producers have structures in their cells—chloroplasts—that use the sun's energy to drive the process of making food. In the presence of light, carbon dioxide (from the air) combines with water (from the soil or air) to produce sugars (carbohydrates) and oxygen. The process can be shown graphically by this equation.

$$CO_2 + H_2O \xrightarrow{\text{light}} C_6H_{12}O_6 + O_2$$

Note how light is not part of the reaction, and thus producers do not make food "from light." Instead, light is the energy that causes the reaction to happen. Producers make sugars (food) to fuel their own life processes and do not need "food," such as fertilizers.

Science and Engineering Practices: Using Mathematics and Computational Thinking

Help dispel misconceptions about the role of light in producing food. Use words to show how photosynthesis occurs in plants: Carbon dioxide plus water yields sugar plus oxygen. Guide students to understand that carbon dioxide is a colorless gas in the air and the waste gas they exhale. Light is the energy that causes this to happen, but light energy does not become the food (sugars) and is instead stored in the food. Water can be present in the soil or air as a gas or a liquid. It is these two materials that react to form sugars and release oxygen. The plant uses some of the sugars itself and stores the rest. The stored sugars feed consumers.

EXPLORE
The Food Machine

Have you ever seen a tree eat a hot dog? Have you ever seen a sunflower eat chips? All plants need food. But they can't eat hot dogs or chips. Plants can't go to a grocery store either. What do they do? They make their own food! Plants are like small food factories. They use sunlight, water, and air to make sugar. Sugar = food. The more food a plant makes, the more it grows. Draw a picture of a weak plant with little sunlight. Next, draw a strong plant and a bright sun. Write a story about these two plants. How did one get so weak and the other so strong?

DIG DEEPER
It's a Blast!

You and your partner are developing a new video game. It's called ChloroBLAST. Here's how it works. You control the sun's energy. Aim carefully. As each plant goes by, zap it! You want the rays to strike the plant's cells. Receive 25 points for each direct hit on a cell. You get another 25 points if you strike the chloroplasts, those small, green, disc-shaped particles found inside the cells—the heart of the plant. Here, chlorophyll, a special ingredient, traps sunlight and supercharges it! This super energy causes the air and water to combine, making the plant's food. It's called "photosynthesis."

This game will soon go on the market. It will be promoted on the Internet and in catalogs. Write an advertisement with three reasons why people should buy this product. Your target audiences are game-players, science teachers, and scientists. Match each reason to the intended audience.

NGSS

2-LS2.A: Interdependent Relationships in Ecosystems

3-LS1.A: Structure and Function

CCSS

W.K.2, W.1.2, W.2.2: Informational Writing

W.3.3, W.4.3, W.5.3: Imaginary Event

ADDITIONAL RESOURCES

Learn with the Ranger how plants travel at http://www.sesamestreet. org Search: "How Plants Travel"

Search on the Internet using terms, such as "germination" for videos like the time-lapse video at http:// easyscienceforkids.com/all-about- germination/ The video is featured at the bottom of the page.

Seeds Go, Seeds Grow by Mark Weakland. Capstone: 2011. (1–2)

Seeds (Plants) by Patricia Whitehouse. Heinemann-Raintree: 2009. (K–2)

LANGUAGE LINK		LEARNING SETTING
Explore:	Informative Writing	Individual
Dig Deeper:	Narrative Writing	Collaboration

Seeds

Science Information

Seeds range greatly in their sizes and shapes (think a coconut versus a poppy seed), but they all have one thing in common—they house the embryo of a new plant. They also include food for the fledgling plant, and a protective coat surrounds most seeds. The fruit that surrounds most seeds is another layer of protection. The fruits also aid in dispersal by wind, water, and animals (think feathery wings and juicy berries).

How old can seeds be and still grow a new plant? That depends on several factors, but the oldest, a small flowering plant, was found encased in Siberian ice and dated at 32,000 years. Others might not survive through one winter. The embryo needs water and air to grow, which can't happen until the seed coat is broken.

Science and Engineering Practices: Planning and Carrying Out Investigations

Supply students with a variety of seeds, such as bean, pea, grapefruit, and orange; small plastic self-sealing bags; paper towels; markers; and water. Guide students to develop a testable question related to seed germination and then use the materials to carry out an investigation to answer the question. They might explore the effects of cold, gravity, orientation, water, light, seed type, soaking versus not soaking, and so on. Guide younger students through the same activity by demonstrating the setup first.

Seeds of Life

You can pick apples from an apple tree.

You can pick beans from a bush.

What do these foods have in common?

They all started as SEEDS! Seeds store food inside of their hard shells. Plant the seed in soil and then water carefully. Soon, your seed may burst wide open. A tiny plant might pop out. Not all seeds produce a plant, and not all seeds are planted by people.

You are walking through a forest. It is so hot! You take off your jacket and drop it on the ground. Later, you find two seeds clinging to the fabric. Let's plant them. Look! From one seed, a tiny wildflower grew. From the other, a blade of grass emerged. Answer this question: "What is another way for seeds to naturally move from place to place?"

....

Ready? Take

DIG DEEPER
Seed Scientists

Imagine finding a 2,000-year-old seed! Scientists have actually discovered seeds as old as this. They had been well preserved in a dry, dusty region. In the science lab, each seed was treated with special care. Would the seed actually germinate, or sprout, after all these years? Finally, the seed coat, or protective outer covering, of one of the seeds actually burst open. A tiny plant emerged. Success! It was a date palm tree.

But now you and your team of scientists have discovered a very strange looking seed. It was found deep inside a dark cave. This seed is much older than all other seeds. What special care do you use to get it to germinate? Draw a picture of this unusual plant, give it a name, and tell the story of how it might have gotten into the cave and survived.

....

Ready? Take

Vertebrates

Science Information

Different animals use their body parts in different ways to move from place to place. Vertebrates are animals that have backbones, which allow for complex nervous systems. A vertebrate's backbone is part of an internal skeletal system that is moved by muscles. Vertebrates are able to move very efficiently. There are over 60,000 vertebrate species. Although this sounds like a lot, it is only about 3 percent of Earth's species. Mammals, birds, reptiles, amphibians and fish are all vertebrates. While they all possess a backbone, they each have defining characteristics.

- Mammals: have fur or hair, feed milk to their young, have lungs, most have young born alive, are "warm blooded" or have a constant body temperature
- Birds: have feathers, have wings (but not necessarily used for flight), lay eggs enclosed in a shell, are "warm blooded" or have a constant body temperature
- Reptiles: have dry, scaly skin; breathe through lungs; most lay eggs enclosed in a shell; are "cold blooded" or have a body temperature that adjusts to the environment
- Amphibians: have moist, smooth skin; breathe through both gills and lungs at different stages; lay eggs enclosed in a membranes; are "cold blooded" or have a body temperature that adjusts to the environment; live part of their lives in water and part on land
- Fish: have skeletons of bone or cartilage, breathe through gills, most lay eggs enclosed in membranes, live in water, have a body temperature that adjusts to the environment, most have scales

PROMPT SUPPLIES

Spine Time	*A Very Vertebrate Mystery*
Science Notebook	
Colored pencils	Science Notebook
	Colored pencils

NGSS

NGSS	CCSS
1-LS1.A: Structure and Function	W.K.1, K.1.1, K.2.1: Support with Facts
4-LS1.A: Structure and Function	W.3.3, W.4.3, W.5.3: Description

ADDITIONAL RESOURCES

Use the word "spine" to search for Internet resources, such as this video at http://easyscienceforkids.com/human-spine-facts-for-kids-video/

Animal School: What Class Are You? Michelle Lord. Holiday House: 2014. (1–3)

Science and Engineering Practices: Making and Using Models

Show students several pictures of vertebrates and invertebrates. For those that it may be difficult to distinguish, such as snakes and earthworms, point out the main differentiating characteristic—the backbone or vertebrae. Challenge students to determine how a backbone allows both flexibility and stability. Give students straws, string, and scissors. Encourage them to make a model of a backbone and demonstrate how it works. Younger students might show this by threading a straw that has been cut into pieces onto a string.

Spine Time

"Sit up straight!"

"Don't slouch."

Has anyone ever heard these words? These are good reminders. They help our backbones stay strong and healthy. Another word for "backbone" is "spine." Our spine has a serious job. It helps hold our bodies upright. It allows us to stand up. It lets our bodies move. Animals with a spine are called "vertebrates." Dogs, fish, and birds are vertebrates. We have a spine. That means we are vertebrates. Is a worm a vertebrate? Explain your answer and provide a drawing to support your answer. Prove your answer.

....

Ready? Take

A Very Vertebrate Mystery

As a team of explorers hack through the underbrush of Taongi Island in the Pacific Ocean, they spy something very unusual. It's like nothing they have every seen. Quickly and quietly they begin taking photographs of this unusual creature. It looks a bit like a bird but also a reptile; yet it also has features of other vertebrates.

As soon as they get a satellite signal, they send the photos back to their base where a team of specialized scientists will examine them carefully. What did they find? Draw a photograph of this unusual vertebrate. It must have at least three features, one from each of the five classes of vertebrates: fish, amphibians, reptiles, birds, and mammals. Label each feature and tell the class from which it comes (example of format: dry, scaly skin: reptile). Next, give this new discovery a name and list other important facts about it based on observations made by the explorers. Possible descriptions could include how it moves, what it eats, and any sounds it makes. Then, describe what happens next to this unsuspecting creature. Is it left alone? Do they capture a specimen to display later? Why?

....

LANGUAGE LINK		LEARNING SETTING
Explore:	Opinion	Individual
Dig Deeper:	Informative Writing	Pair

Invertebrates

Science Information

Invertebrates are animals that don't have backbones. Surprisingly, 97 percent of all species are invertebrates. Invertebrates use their body parts in different ways to move. Spiders and crabs move via muscles connected to their hard outer skeletons. Mollusks, like squids and scallops, eject water from their bodies or shells to move. Worms push or pull themselves by stretching and contracting their muscles. It is estimated that there are well over a million species of invertebrates. The main classes are sponges, cnidaria (corals and jellies), flatworms (tapeworms), roundworms, segmented worms (earthworms), arthropods (insects, spiders, and crustaceans), mollusks (clams, squid, and snails), and echinoderms (sea stars and urchins).

Science and Engineering Practices: Engaging in Argument from Evidence

Show students pictures of various invertebrates—sponges, cnidaria, flatworms, roundworms, segmented worms, arthropods, mollusks, and echinoderms—found through a keyword search, such as "invertebrates kinds." Have students share the general characteristics of the example(s) they observe and cite evidence for the claim that they are invertebrates.

PROMPT SUPPLIES

INteresting INvertebrates

Science Notebook

Name Game

Science Notebook

NGSS

1-LS1.A: Structure and Function

5-LS1.C: Organization for Matter and Energy Flow in Organisms

CCSS

W.K.3, W.1.3, W.2.3: Support with Reasons

W.3.2.A, W.4.2.A, W.5.2.A: Grouping

ADDITIONAL RESOURCES

Follow Bill Nye the Science Guy as he explores "Invertebrates." This video is available on the Internet.

Photographs of unusual invertebrates can be found on the Internet at websites, such as http://www.arkive.org/invertebrates-terrestrial-and-freshwater/

Classifying Invertebrates by Francine Galko. Heinemann-Raintree: 2009. (3–5)

Invertebrates by Angela Royston. Heinemann-Raintree: 2015. (1–3)

INteresting INvertebrates

You are a vertebrate. How do we know? You have a spine, or backbone. An invertebrate does not have a backbone. But here are some invertebrate facts many people don't know!

Grasshoppers have ears on their stomachs.

An earthworm can grow to 10 feet (3 meters) long!

Lobster and shrimp have 10 legs.

Butterflies can taste food with their feet.

Ants can lift objects 50 times their body weight.

Some jellyfish can glow in the dark.

What if you had one of these invertebrate features? Which one would you like to have? How would you use it?

Ready? Take 5!

Name Game

Almost 97 percent of all animal species are invertebrates. But what else do they have in common? Take a look at these common invertebrates.

earthworm   jellyfish   snail   octopus   spider   ant

bee   grasshopper   clam   butterfly   sea star   sponge

So what characteristics do some of these 12 organisms have in common? You and your partner are to think of different ways to group two or more of these organisms. For example, you might have classification headings, such as "soft outer bodies" or "invertebrates that swim or crawl or fly." In other words, let your own imagination fly as you search for common characteristics among these invertebrates. What about "Creepy Crawlers" or "Stinging Defenders"?

Ready? Take

PROMPT SUPPLIES

A Visit to a Castle

Science Notebook

Save the Queen

Science Notebook

NGSS

1-LS1.A: Structure and Function

4-LS1.D: Information Processing

CCSS

L.K.5.A, L.1.5.A, L.2.5.A: Sorting

W.3.3, W.4.3, W.5.3: Descriptive Details

ADDITIONAL RESOURCES

Learn about the unique senses of a hammerhead shark in at http://www.animalplanet.com Search: "senses"

What's the sixth sense? This animated cartoon tells all: http://www.pbs.org/parents/wildkratts/activities/discovering-senses/

Amazing Animal Senses by John Townsend. Heinemann-Raintree: 2012. (1–3)

Using Your Senses by Rebecca Rissman. Heinemann-Raintree: 2011. (PreK–1)

LANGUAGE LINK		LEARNING SETTING
Explore:	Vocabulary	Individual
Dig Deeper:	Narrative Writing	Individual

The Senses

Science Information

Sense organs allow organisms to interact with their environments. Observations, gathered by the senses, are processed by the brain. The brain compares the new data with previous observations and acts accordingly. Sense organs and the senses themselves vary among different animal groups. Ears and eyes are common and receive sound and light energy of various intensities and wavelengths. Sensors for taste, however, might be on the tongue of a mammal or the feet and antennae of insects! Some animals go beyond the typical five senses and can sense electrical and magnetic fields.

Science and Engineering Practices: Using Mathematics and Computational Thinking

Students might devise a graph to depict the sensory observations they made in the course of a day using each of their senses—sight, hearing, taste, smell, and touch. They can determine what kind of graph is most appropriate to display their data.

A Visit to a Castle

Look closely at the photograph. Now use your imagination. Step into the picture. Walk around and enjoy the view. Listen carefully. Take a deep breath. It is time to explore with your five senses. Make five lines going down your paper. At the top of each column write these labels: "I See," "I Hear," "I Smell," "I Taste," and "I Touch." Under these labels, draw or write your responses. Place at least two responses in each column. Then answer this question: "Would you like to live here? Why or why not?" Include your senses to explain your answer.

Ready? Take 5!

Save the Queen

Oh no! The queen has been kidnapped! It is up to you to slip into the enemy's castle and rescue her. You have been chosen because you are a very unusual being. You have very sharp senses, like those of many animals. Answer these questions in the correct sequence. Narrate what you do first, second, next, and so on.

1. You are approaching the castle. How will you use the sense of hearing? (Note: dogs can hear higher pitches of sound than humans.)

2. You have made it to the castle wall. How will you use your magnetic sense? This is like a built-in compass. (Note: This sense is used by migratory birds flying north or south.)

3. There is a doorway up ahead. How will you use your infrared sense? (Note: Snakes use this to detect "warm-blooded" prey.)

4. At last! You are inside the castle. Now it's time to use your sense of smell. [Note: Bears can smell food 18 miles (29 kilometers) away]. How will this help?

Continue your search and rescue of the queen using at least two more senses. This could include taste, touch, sight, echolocation, ultraviolet senses, and any other special animal senses.

Ready? Take

Hibernation

Science Information

Organisms have many strategies to meet their needs in a relatively stable web of life. When food becomes scarce, many organisms move to another area where food is available. Others stay where they are and hibernate until food is available—usually during the winter. In this sleeplike state, their metabolic rate and body temperature are reduced, which reduces the need for food. Animals that hibernate build up fat in their bodies prior to winter, which supplies energy during hibernation. Skunks, prairie dogs, bats, and common poorwills are only a few of the many animals that hibernate. While bears are often described as hibernating in winter, their activity level varies, and females give birth during the winter months.

Some animals, such as amphibians, are said to hibernate in the summer. While similar to hibernation, this period of inactivity is to escape the heat by resting in a cool, moist place for shorter periods of time.

Science and Engineering Practices: Obtaining, Evaluating, and Communicating Information

Describe hibernation as a deep sleep that lasts for several weeks. Elicit from students their ideas about how that sleep would change the animal's needs. Would it need more or less food and water? What kind of "bed" would it prepare? Where would the bed need to be? Would the animal be alone or with others? Follow each question with "why" to encourage reasoning skills.

PROMPT SUPPLIES

Bats, Box Turtles & Bees	*The Lonely Queen*
Science Notebook	Science Notebook

NGSS

1-LS1.B Growth and Development of Organisms

1-LS1.D: Information Processing

4-LS1.A: Structure and Function

CCSS

W.K.1, W.1.1, W.2.1: Support with Reasons

W.3.3, W.4.3, W.5.3: Descriptive Details

ADDITIONAL RESOURCES

Learn about the hibernating habits of different animals in Yellowstone National Park at http://www.nps.gov/index.htm Search: "Inside Yellowstone hibernation"

Colorful video footage and special effects follow the preparations of a chipmunk getting ready to hibernate at http://www.discovery.com/ Search: "Chipmunk"

"The Groundhog Song" sets a lively pace as animals prepare for the coming winter at http://www.watchknowlearn.org/ Search: "The Groundhog Song"

Animal Hibernation by Jeanie Mebane. Capstone: 2012. (1–3)

999 Frogs Wake Up by Ken Kimura. NorthSouth: 2013. (K–2)

Bats, Box Turtles & Bees

On a very cold night you snuggle into your bed. A blanket keeps you safe and warm. Bats, box turtles, and a bumblebee queen don't have a blanket. A deep, deep sleep keeps them safe and warm! A bat can sleep for 2 months. A box turtle can sleep for 4 months. A queen bee can sleep for 6 to 8 months! Sleep helps them survive the cold. This is called "hibernation." Do you think people should hibernate? Why or why not? State your opinion and write two reasons to support it.

Ready? Take

The Lonely Queen

Some animals hibernate in groups to stay nice and warm to survive cold temperatures. In fact, hundreds of garter snakes usually hibernate together! But think of the lonely bumblebee queen. After all the worker bees in a nest die, she alone will hibernate to survive a cold winter. She may burrow into a tree stump or dig into the ground until spring arrives. Then, she is off to find food and a new nest to lay her eggs.

While being a queen might sound like a grand idea, one queen is unhappy with her life. She is quite lonely. She has kept a diary of her life detailing events in the hive before, during, and after hibernation. Let's take a peek. Create three diary entries for the queen. Be sure to include the word "hibernation" in two entries.

Ready? Take

Migration

Science Information

Migration aids survival. Zebra populations follow Africa's pattern of rainfall as the rains sweep in a circle of over 300 miles (nearly 500 kilometers). Follow the rain or stay and die where it's dry. Monarch butterflies migrate to central Mexico from many parts of the United States. Some turtles cross thousands of miles (kilometers) of open ocean to lay their eggs below beaches that are just the right temperature. Whales, who travel the greatest distances of any migrators, swim from food-rich cold waters near the Arctic to warmer water nearer the equator to give birth. Many salmon species are born in rivers and streams but swim to oceans for the abundant food found there. When they mature, these same fish travel to the distant places of their birth to spawn and die.

Science and Engineering Practices: Asking Questions and Defining Problems

Record questions from students about migration. How is navigation done? What does migration say about how Earth's habitats are connected? What happens when we change habitats? What adaptations make some animals successful migrators? Record these questions and discuss with students which might be answered through experimentation and which might be best answered through research.

PROMPT SUPPLIES

Duck, Duck, Goose!	*Red Crabs of Christmas Island*
Science Notebook	Science Notebook
Colored pencils	

NGSS	CCSS
1-LS1.A: Structure and Function	W.K.2, W.1.2, W.2.2: Support with Facts
3-LS4.C: Adaptation	W.3.2.B, W.4.2.B, W.5.2.B: Support with Examples
4-LS4.C: Adaptation	
For any particular environment, some kinds of organisms survive well, some survive less well, and some cannot survive at all. (3-LS4.3)	

ADDITIONAL RESOURCES

Junior Naturalist Patrice takes young viewers on a journey into migration at http://video.nhptv.org/video/1491137382/

Watch the fascinating march of red crabs to the sea at http://www.animalplanet.com/ Search: "red crab"

Animal Migration by Jeanie Mebane. Capstone: 2012. (1–2)

Great Migrations by K.M. Kostyal. National Geographic: 2010. (1–3)

Duck, Duck, Goose!

Whitney and her grandmother have gone for a walk one fall day.

Her grandmother shivered. "It's starting to get cool," she said.

Suddenly, they saw a large flock of ducks overhead.

Grandmother observed, "The ducks are migrating south. They don't like the cold either."

"Hey," Whitney said. "You fly south for the winter, too."

Whitney's grandmother migrates to a warmer climate in the winter. There, she takes long walks and swims in the pool. But what about ducks? What do they do?

Draw three boxes on your paper.

In the first box, draw the ducks migrating south. In the second box, draw the ducks enjoying themselves in their winter home. In the third box, answer this question: "Why don't all animals migrate?"

Ready? Take

Red Crabs of Christmas Island

Monarch butterflies migrate, or travel, thousands of miles (kilometers) south to escape Canada's cold winters. Elk migrate to greener pastures for food. The famous Christmas Island red crabs migrate to reproduce. Millions of red crabs will scuttle out of the rainforest of this small island in the Indian Ocean. After mating, the females will wait in their burrows before heading to the water to lay their eggs. They remain in their burrows until their red offspring emerge from the sea. Then, they return to the rainforest.

Not all of these animals will survive the return journey. What kinds of obstacles might any of these animals face to prevent them from returning home? List each animal species and any threats to its safety.

Ready? Take

©2016 Kaye Hagler and Judy Elgin Jensen from *Take 5! for Science*. This page may be reproduced for classroom use only.

Just Like Me!

Science
Notebook

Colored pencils

It's in Your Genes

Science
Notebook

Colored pencils

NGSS

1-LS3.A:
Inheritance
of Traits

3-LS3.A:
Inheritance
of Traits

CCSS

W.K.2, W.1.2,
W.2.2: Support
with Examples

W.3.2.B, W.4.2.B,
W.5.2.B: Support
with Examples

ADDITIONAL RESOURCES

Tim and Moby explore heredity at
https://www.brainpop.com/health/
geneticsgrowthanddevelopment/
heredity/

Looking for an introduction to
DNA? The first half of this video
can lead to further discussions:
http://ed.ted.com/lessons/the-
twisting-tale-of-dna-judith-hauck

DNA and Heredity by Casey Rand.
Heinemann-Raintree: 2010. (4–6)

LANGUAGE LINK		LEARNING SETTING
Explore:	Informative Writing	Individual
Dig Deeper:	Informative Writing	Individual

Heredity

Science Information

Physical traits each individual sees when one looks in the mirror are
inherited from his or her biological parents. Traits are controlled
by genes, which are segments of DNA that have been passed
from parent to offspring. It is the DNA that determines the kind
of organism one is. Genes control specific traits, from physical
features (four legs and a tail) to chemical components (skin color)
to behaviors (web building). The effects of genes can vary. The slight
differences are called "variations." Determining the structure of the
DNA molecule was a major scientific breakthrough of the mid-20th
century. The molecule resembles a twisted ladder with deoxyribose
sugar molecules as the sides and rungs composed of nucleic acids—
thus DNA.

Science and Engineering Practices: Using Mathematics and Computational Thinking

Any given classroom contains combinations of just about any
physical feature imaginable. Have students devise a list of physical
features to be surveyed and a suitable graph with which to share
class data. Students might survey features, such as eye color, hair
color, or hair texture. Guide students to differentiate between
environmental effects on traits and the original appearance of the
trait. For example, dark hair that has been lightened by the sun is a
trait that would be passed along to offspring as dark hair.

Just Like Me!

Visitors to the zoo were so excited. They were going to the animal nursery. First, they saw the cute panda cub. It had large black eyes and white fur. It looked just like its parents. Next, they saw a small zebra. It had black and white stripes. It looked just like its parents. These traits had been passed down, or inherited, from their parents. This is called "heredity." Heredity passes down features from the parents to their babies. These features can be inherited:

The color of your hair   How tall or short you are

The color of your eyes   Long or short fingers

The color of your skin   Other trait?

Now, draw a picture of yourself. Use the list above to label at least five traits you think are inherited.

....

Ready? Take

©2016 Kaye Hagler and Judy Elgin Jensen from *Take 5! for Science.* This page may be reproduced for classroom use only.

DIG DEEPER
It's in Your Genes

Who do you look like? People inherit traits that have been passed down from their parents. These traits determine what they look like. Each cell in our body carries instructions that determine what we look like. These are our genes. Genes are strung together in long strands. Our genes determine traits, such as our hair and skin color, and whether we will be short or tall. Genes operate like a code. What do they look like?

Draw a twisted ladder. On each rung of the ladder you will be writing a code like VT (very tall) or BH (brown hair). Think of at least five traits to describe yourself and give each trait a code. Place these codes all along the rungs. Beneath your illustration, provide a key for the codes.

....

Ready? Take

Adaptation and Change

Science Information

In everyday language, humans readily adapt to new situations—an unexpected visitor for instance. In science, the term "adapt" refers to gene changes that occur over long periods of time. In any group of organisms of the same kind, the exact way a gene expresses itself will differ slightly from one individual to the next. If the slight difference, or variation, helps the individual survive and reproduce, it will pass along that exact gene. For example, a polar bear with slightly more body fat than other polar bears would have a slightly better chance of surviving and reproducing.

Organisms do not develop new variations when a change happens in the environment. But those who already have a certain variation might be better able to survive the change. Over time, that exact gene will become more common, and will be described as an adaptation.

Science and Engineering Practices: Planning and Carrying Out Investigations

Supply students with plastic bags, shortening, rubber bands, rulers, and large containers of very cold water. Challenge them to demonstrate how variations in the amount of blubber a whale has affects whether the whale will survive in frigid arctic waters. Students can cover both hands with a plastic bag held snugly at the wrist with a rubber band. By adding layers of shortening of various thicknesses to one or both hands, covering with a second plastic bag held snugly at the wrist, and holding their hands in very cold water for several seconds, students can collect data for analysis to support claims.

PROMPT SUPPLIES

Being Special	*It's Not Magic; It's Adaptation!*
Science Notebook	Science Notebook

NGSS	CCSS
1-LS1.B: Growth and Development of Organisms	W.K.3, W.1.3, W.2.3: Imagined Experiences
3-LS4.B: Natural Selection	W.3.3, W.4.3, W.5.3: Imagined Experiences

ADDITIONAL RESOURCES

How do beavers adapt to their environment? Discover this and more at http://video.nhptv.org/video/1492015101

Search the Internet for videos about animal adaptations and how they allow animals to survive. Search "zebra stripes" at animalplanet.com/ to find information that links zebras' stripes to their survival.

Amazing Animal Adaptations, a four-book set, by Lisa J. Amstutz, Julie Murphy. Capstone: 2011. (1–2)

Bonobos by Buffy Silverman. Heinemann-Raintree: 2012. (3–6)

Being Special

Brrr! It's cold. Too bad you're not a penguin. Penguins don't need jackets. They have a layer of fat under their skin. It keeps them warm in the winter.

You are thirsty, but there's no water nearby. Too bad you're not a wood rat. They get their water from eating food like a cactus.

These animals have features that help them live in their environments. We call these "adaptations." These adaptations help them survive in their habitats. Some adaptations help animals blend into their surroundings, carry their own water supply, fly, or wear a thick shaggy coat.

What special adaptations would you like to have? Tell a story about how they would help you during a typical day. You may add a drawing to help support your response.

....

It's Not Magic; It's Adaptation!

Chopping down 200 trees a year with just your front teeth is a tough job. If you are a beaver, no worries! A beaver's front teeth, or incisors, NEVER stop growing. They may wear down, but they keep growing and growing. Beavers will use limbs from fallen trees to create a lodge. This lodge-building behavior is an adaptation. In their lodge, beavers are safe from predators.

Choose three of the following adaptations and write a story about how they help you overcome a real-life challenge:

- the teeth of a beaver that never stop growing
- the transparent eyelids of a beaver
- the puffer fish's ability to suddenly inflate like a balloon
- the quill-covered body of a porcupine
- the ability to suddenly change colors like a chameleon

NGSS

1-LS1.B:
Growth and
Development
of Organisms

4-LS1.A:
Structure and
Function

CCSS

W.K.2, W.1.2,
W.2.2: Support
with Facts

W.3.2.A,
W.4.2.A, W.5.2.A:
Grouping

ADDITIONAL RESOURCES

Fascinating footage reveals
more about the lives of
dolphins and bears at:

- http://www.discovery.com/tv-
  shows/north-america/videos/
  clever-dolphins-hunt-together/

- http://www.discovery.com/
  tv-shows/north-america/
  videos/baby-black-bear-
  learns-the-ropes/

Doing what comes naturally,
this series of videos features
various animal behaviors: http://
animals.nationalgeographic.com/
animals/crittercam-wildcam/

All About Animals, a four-book set, by
Tammy Gagne. Capstone: 2015. (1–2)

Learn About Animal Behavior, a
four-book set, by Kelli L. Hicks,
Jeanie Mebane, Kelsi Turner
Tjernagel. Capstone: 2012. (1–2)

LANGUAGE LINK		LEARNING SETTING
Explore:	Informative Writing	Individual
Dig Deeper:	Informative Writing	Individual

Behavior

Science Information

Behaviors are the sum of actions that an organism performs. Plants, animals, and other kinds of organisms exhibit behaviors. Often one thinks of animal behaviors, such as web-building or herding. Plants, however, also show behaviors, or growth patterns, in terms of how they respond to certain environmental conditions, such as light and water. Many behaviors are built-in as stimulus-response reactions. They could be thought of as "hard wired" in genes. Yet many animals' behaviors are learned through trial-and-error, imprinting, conditioning, and insight. So while the ability to learn is determined by genes, the particular actions that are learned are based on experiences in the environment.

Science and Engineering Practices: Using Mathematics and Computational Thinking

Challenge students to name behaviors and then determine the cause-and-effect relationships that might result in those behaviors. Encourage them to diagram the relationships as sequence or flow charts. For example, they might describe a dog that stands by its food bowl at the same time each day or a school of fish that swims around in tight circles when a predator comes near.

Behave Yourself!

Animals like cats and monkeys nurse their babies. This is a behavior. The milk helps them grow.

A mother penguin leaves her nest. She must hunt for food. Daddy penguin stays behind to keep the eggs warm. This is also a behavior.

A mother whale swims beside her baby calf. She pushes it to the surface. Here, the baby will take a deep breath. Then back under the water it goes.

These are all called "behaviors." These actions help parents care for their babies. Write or draw two other behaviors of animals. Beside each, answer this question: "How does the behavior help the animal live and grow?" Example: Birds fly in flocks. Why? To search for food and for safety.

Ready? Take 5!

DIG DEEPER
Act Naturally

Why do they do that? When an enemy is stalking a prey, sometimes it is safer to be with a group. Many animals in the wild run in packs, prides, or herds. This behavior provides protection for them.

Running with the pack can also help in obtaining food. Of course, if you are a lion cub, you will have to wait your turn. The youngest or weakest are last to eat. This is another animal behavior.

It's time for another field trip! Our jeep will slowly drive through a natural preserve where animals from around the world can be spotted. Here, we will see animals running in packs and obtaining their food. We will probably see a baby giraffe walking close behind its mother or a lion stalking its prey. Take a picture (create a drawing) for the family photo album showing two other behaviors we might observe in a nature preserve or zoo and provide a description.

Ready? Take

Endangered Species

Science Information

Our Fish and Wildlife Service has been protecting endangered animals and plants since 1973. Species identified as "endangered" are likely to become extinct if nothing changes. Although these species are still here, there is no guarantee about their futures even though efforts are being made to protect them. The main threats to endangered species are climate change, habitat loss, illegal wildlife trade, natural resource development, unrestricted harvesting, and pollution. All of these threats result from human activities.

Science and Engineering Practices: Obtaining, Evaluating, and Communicating Information

Facilitate students' Internet research by logging onto http://www.fws.gov/endangered/. There, students can discover endangered species in their home states or others. They can extend their investigation to their local area by contacting local wildlife support groups. Have them conclude their research with a short presentation or poster about endangered species—what they are, why species become endangered, the most common threats, and ways people might help.

PROMPT SUPPLIES

Save the Turtles	*Cut It Out!*
Science Notebook	Science Notebook
Colored pencils	

NGSS	CCSS
2-LS4.D: Biodiversity and Humans	W.K.1, W.1.1, W.2.1: Support with Reasons
3-LS4.C: Adaptation	W.3.1.C, W.4.1.C, W.5.1.C: Support with Reasons

ADDITIONAL RESOURCES

What efforts are being made to save endangered species? Find out at http://www.pbslearningmedia.org Search: "Endangered Species"

Want to adopt a crocodile? See what one person can do to help save an endangered species at http://www.kidsplanet.org/factsheets/map.html

Can We Save the Tiger? by Martin Jenkins. Candlewick Press: 2011. (K–3)

Safari Survival: Volume 5 by Jan Burchett, Sara Vogler. Stone Arch Books: 2013. (3–6)

Save the Turtles

Dr. Ross is a special doctor. He does not treat people. He treats turtles! Today, he is giving a large leatherback sea turtle a shot of medicine. This turtle is very sick. Dr. Ross is worried about all leatherback sea turtles. They are disappearing. Many get caught in fishing nets and die. New homes built along the beach and beach erosion have destroyed many of the turtles' nesting sites. Now, these turtles are an endangered species. One day, they may all disappear! What can we do to help these turtles survive? Create a poster. Persuade people they can help leatherback sea turtles survive. Include two specific actions.

Ready? Take **5!**

Cut It Out!

In 1973, Congress passed the Endangered Species Act. It defined an endangered species as a "species which is in danger of extinction throughout all or a significant portion of its range . . ."

Uh-oh! You have a problem. As director of the Endangered Species Program, you have to cut millions of dollars from your budget.

You must reduce the funding for one of the areas below. Which will it be and why?

1. Staffing to monitor and list endangered species

2. Legal services to challenge and defend efforts/individuals that hinder conservation efforts

3. Purchasing lands

4. Recovery efforts to build an endangered species population

It's a tough job. You will need to write an e-mail to your staff. Explain your choice and your reasons. Use two of the following words or phrases: "because," "consequently," "for instance," "in order to," or "therefore."

ADDITIONAL RESOURCES

An abundance of guide sheets about fossils are available at the Brooklyn Children's Museum at http://www.brooklynkids.org/attachments/fossils_fin_hr.pdf

In this unique lab, older students will appreciate the information provided in each step to create their own fossil with the "Fossil Fabricator" at http://www.wonderville.ca/asset/fossil-fabricator

Interesting information on fossils can be found at http://www.fossilsforkids.com/

Figuring Out Fossils by Sally M. Walker. Lerner: 2013. (3–4)

Fossil by Claire Ewart. Walker Childrens: 2014. (K–3)

Fossils by Richard Spilsbury and Louise Spilsbury. Heinemann-Raintree: 2011. (3–6)

LANGUAGE LINK		LEARNING SETTING
Explore:	Informative Writing	Individual
Dig Deeper:	Opinion	Individual

Fossils

Science Information

Fossils are either impressions of once living organisms or traces left behind by the actions of living things. They might be impressions (or molds) or materials that fill in the impression and then break away (casts). Sometimes they are the actual thing itself, such as an insect trapped in amber. Bones and woody parts can undergo chemical change when they are buried in soil and minerals seep in and replace the cells, as in petrified wood.

Fossils provide the record that scientists need to learn about life from the past. The United Kingdom's *Independent*, a news source, reported that the "oldest" fossil ever found was in Australia. Scientists from Old Dominion University claim their find is 3.5 billion years old! Recently fossilized human footprints, dated 950,000 years old, were found in England.

Science and Engineering Practices: Obtaining, Evaluating, and Communicating Information

Direct students to or show them one or more of the many animations of fossil formation on the Internet. Challenge them to describe in their own words what the video is showing. They might frame their descriptions as a series of numbered steps or a narrative about what happened. If they viewed several animations, they could add notes about which they thought best communicated the information.

Uncovering the Past

Roja and Maneli were hiking through the woods.

"Look at this rock!" Roja said.

Maneli looked closely. "That's not just a rock. That's a fossil!"

How does she know? First, list two possible clues she might have seen.

You also want to find a fossil. Where might be a good starting place? The seashore? A stream? Your backyard? Explain your answer.

Ready? Take

Up for Grabs

A very unusual fossil has just been discovered. It looks like a small flying insect or maybe a tiny bird. It is embedded in a rock. One thing is certain. It is very old, maybe as old as the earliest dinosaurs. Scientists are anxious to study it. What information will it reveal, they wonder. So who gets it first?

The paleontologist studies plants and animals preserved in rocks that lived long ago, even before the dinosaurs. She loves to dig for fossils.

The geologist studies materials of Earth. "Geo" means "earth." He would love to examine those minerals. They might hold clues to Earth's earliest history.

A zoologist studies not only present-day animals but also the development of animals from the their earliest beginnings. Is this creature the first stage of a modern animal?

You get to decide. Who will get first crack at this fossil? Give two reasons to defend your decision.

Ready? Take

Extinction

Science Information

Carl Sagan once said, "Extinction is the rule. Survival is the exception." Sagan refers to the fact that in the historical record, more species have permanently disappeared than are here now. That occurred due to natural changes in Earth's history. Today, the World Wildlife Fund estimates that somewhere between 10,000 and 100,000 species are becoming extinct every year. And unless future technologies create a way, they will never come back.

Species on the endangered list, however, can still come back from the brink. They need not disappear forever if appropriate actions are taken and maintained because many current extinctions are human caused.

Science and Engineering Practices: Asking Questions and Defining Problems

Students know that dinosaurs are extinct as are woolly mammoths and saber-toothed cats. They might even know that dodo birds and passenger pigeons are extinct. But what about animals today? Elicit from students questions they have about extinctions and extinction rates that might be investigated through research. Examples might include research to be conducted on what is extinct today in the wild, what is living only in zoos, why animals are going extinct today, or why plants are going extinct too.

PROMPT SUPPLIES

Disappearing Birds	*Digging Up Dinosaurs*
Science Notebook	Science Notebook

NGSS	CCSS
2-LS4.D: Biodiversity and Humans	W.K.2, W.1.2, W.2.2: Support with Facts
3-LS4.A: Evidence of Common Ancestry and Diversity	W.3.1, W.4.2, W.5.3: Support with Reasons

ADDITIONAL RESOURCES

Search the Internet for Time's photo essay of "Ten Species Near Extinction"

What animals may soon become extinct? Go to http://www.dailymotion.com Search: "10 animals that may go extinct in the next 10 years"

Mission: Lion Rescue: All About Lions and How to Save Them by Ashlee Brown Blewett. National Geographic Children's Books: 2014. (5+)

Small and Tall Tales of Extinct Animals by Damien Laverdunt. Lerner: 2012. (3–6)

Disappearing Birds

A long time ago, billions of birds called "passenger pigeons" flew across the sky. Their flocks were huge. They would block out the sun as they flew by. They were the largest group of birds found anywhere in the world. People enjoyed hunting and eating these plentiful birds. And so they hunted and hunted and hunted. Finally, not a single passenger pigeon was left. They became extinct. Many other birds are in danger. Their habitats are being destroyed by the construction of homes and buildings. Some hunters kill them for sport and not just food. Also, new animals are being brought into their habitats. These native birds cannot defend themselves against these predators. How can we help birds survive? Explain two ways.

Ready? Take

Digging Up Dinosaurs

A popular movie once described a world where dinosaurs were brought back from extinction and kept on a remote island. Today, some scientists are exploring this real-life possibility. They want to extract DNA, the code of life found in all cells, from fossilized dinosaur bones. Some scientists think the fossils are too old for any experiments. Still, research is in progress to see if the impossible can one day become possible. What do you think? Should time and money be spent to bring back extinct animals, or should time and money be spent to protect current endangered species? Provide two reasons to support your opinion.

Ready? Take

Properties Sound States of Matter

Atoms Magnets Friction Energy

Chemical Reaction Heat Speed

Motion Mass Mixtures Physical Change

Color Opaque Solutions Light Conductors Waves Vibrations

Insulators

Temperature

Translucent Electricity Force

Matter Molecules

Weight Velocity

Transparent

Chapter 4:
Physical Science Prompts

Break It Down!

Science
Notebook

Colored pencils

All Charged Up!

Science
Notebook

Cup of water

Pipette or
eyedropper

Coin or small
round disks

NGSS

2-PS1.A:
Structure and
Properties
of Matter

5-PS1.A:
Structure and
Properties
of Matter

CCSS

W.K.1, W.1.1,
W.2.1: Support
with Reasons

W.3.3, W.4.3,
W.5.3: Imagined
Experience

ADDITIONAL RESOURCES

A grapefruit as big as Earth? Check
out this and other analogies
at http://ed.ted.com/lessons/
just-how-small-is-an-atom

"Bill Nye The Science Guy & Atoms"
can be found on the Internet.

*Frank Einstein and the Antimatter
Motor: Book One* by Jon
Scieszka and Brian Biggs. Harry
N. Abrams: 2014. (2–6)

Ghosts and Atoms by Jodi Wheeler-
Toppen. Capstone: 2011. (3–4)

LANGUAGE LINK		LEARNING SETTING
Explore:	Opinion	Individual
Dig Deeper:	Narrative Writing	Pair

Atoms and Molecules

Science Information

Democritus, a Greek philosopher, first thought of atoms around 600 BCE. His reasoning involved breaking a lump of matter in half. He asked himself what would happen if he kept breaking it in half until he couldn't break it any more. Democritus thought the smallest possible particle, which might be too small to see, would be an atom. We now know that atoms are made of even smaller particles. A current definition of an atom is that it's the smallest particle of an element that has the chemical properties of that element. Almost 120 different types of atoms have been identified that have different observable properties, although around 30 exist only in laboratories. Atoms can be thought of as the building blocks that make up all matter, existing independently or joining with themselves or other atoms as molecules.

Science and Engineering Practices: Obtaining, Evaluating, and Communicating Information

Even today, atoms are invisible except through the most powerful microscopes. Given that, how are people to understand the structure and function of atoms? Have students suggest what kinds of sources they would look in for evidence related to atoms— science books? Encyclopedias? Television shows? Challenge them to explain why they think that particular source is credible. As an analogy, younger students might observe an everyday classroom object, such as a desk or a notebook, and list the individual pieces from which it is made. They could then make a claim about what might happen if one of the pieces were removed from the object.

EXPLORE
Break It Down!

In class, Drey's teacher gave each student a few grains of sand and a magnifying class. The magnifying glass made each tiny grain of sand explode in size! Draw one large grain of sand. But Drey and his class could not see all the tiny pieces joined together to make the grain of sand. Let's add them to the drawing. Create very small circles along the outside and on the inside of your grain of sand. Make them as tiny as you can! Sometimes people call these tiny pieces building blocks. Explain why.

DIG DEEPER
All Charged Up!

With your partner, observe the cup of water. What's inside? Water! Now use the dropper or pipette to place a small drop of water onto the coin. What do you see? Water! Now place another drop of water on the coin. Instead of two drops, you now see one bigger drop. Atoms are building blocks. Three atoms join together to make one water molecule—two atoms of hydrogen and one of oxygen. Another way to express this is H_2O. Each water molecule then acts like a magnet. It attracts other water molecules, and so the drop gets bigger and bigger. Now, add two more drops. Even bigger? But what if a water molecule refused to join another molecule like a stubborn oil molecule? What would that conversation be like? Provide at least two science-based reasons in the dialogue between these two molecules.

PROMPT SUPPLIES

It's Elemental	*If You Were an Element*
Science Notebook	Science Notebook

NGSS

2-PS1.A: Structure and Properties of Matter

5-PS1.A: Structure and Properties of Matter

CCSS

L.K.5.A, L.1.5.A, L.2.5.A: Sorting

W.3.1.B, W.4.1.B, W.5.1.B: Support with Reasons

ADDITIONAL RESOURCES

Search "Periodic Table" at various websites, including http://www.sciencechannel.com/ so that students can learn more about elements.

Periodic Table printables are available from many websites, including the Jefferson Lab website at http://education.jlab.org/itselemental/

Get ready to move when you "Meet the Elements" at http://www.primarygames.com/videos/category/science/tmbg-meet-the-elements/

Basher Science: The Complete Periodic Table: All the Elements with Style by Adrian Dingle and Simon Basher. Kingfisher: 2015. (5–9)

LANGUAGE LINK	
Explore:	Vocabulary
Dig Deeper:	Opinion

LEARNING SETTING
Individual
Individual

Elements

Science Information

Your chair, the desk, and the paper you are reading from are made of atoms. There are more than 100 different types of atoms, and each different type is an element. Each element has its own name, such as carbon, and a one- or two-letter symbol, such as C. Scientists have grouped the elements into a pattern based on characteristics of the elements to create the periodic table. Elements in the table are grouped according to atomic number and chemical properties. Elements are grouped in rows (known as periods) based on how their arrangement of electrons ascends. Columns display elements that have very similar chemical properties because they have the same arrangement of electrons.

Science and Engineering Practices: Asking Questions and Defining Problems

Students are most engaged when they investigate answers to questions or solve problems of their own choosing but sometimes need a springboard. As students view the Nova video CHNOPS: Ingredients for Life (available by typing CHNOPS in the search box at pbs.org), have them make a list of questions to discuss as a class after watching the video. The questions could be collected on the board, and teams could choose which they might investigate through an experiment or research. Guide younger students to simply say which might be answered by looking in books or by doing experiments.

EXPLORE
It's Elemental

Science has a special definition for an element. It is material that can't be broken down. Think of Dorothy's friend in *The Wizard of Oz*—the Tin Man. He was tin all the way from top to bottom. Tin is an element in science. Today you are going to an amusement park. As you walk along, keep your eyes open. We are going to play "I Spy an Element." Look! There's a statue of the Tin Man, and it's made of tin. That's one element. Look! There is an iron bar in the monkey bars. Iron is an element. Do you see any nickel, aluminum, gold, iron, helium, or neon? Those are also elements. Find at least two elements in the park and tell how each is used.

DIG DEEPER
If You Were an Element

What is the simplest form of matter? An element.

What cannot be broken down? An element.

How are elements represented? By letters. Al is the abbreviation for Aluminum; O stands for Oxygen.

What is a compound? Two or more elements joined together.

Sodium Chloride = two elements Na (Sodium) + Cl (Chlorine) = Table Salt

Got it? Now, it's your turn. Identify yourself as an element (a single letter). Attach at least two more elements to yourself to make a compound. Identify each element with letters like GW (Game Wizard) or LR (Love Reading). Under the representation, explain why these elements best identify you. What do these symbols and the abbreviations for chemical elements have in common?

PROMPT SUPPLIES

What's the Matter?

Science Notebook

Assorted objects

Five Questions

Science Notebook

Blindfold (optional)

Assorted objects

NGSS

2-PS1.A: Structure and Properties of Matter

5-PS1.A: Structure and Properties of Matter

CCSS

L.K.5.A, L.1.5.A, L.2.6: Sorting

SL.3.3, SL.4.1.C, SL.5.1.C: Asking Questions

ADDITIONAL RESOURCES

Bring STEM into the classroom at http://www.sesamestreet. org Search: "Classroom STEM: Properties of Matter"

Bill Nye the Science Guy has all the answers for "Phases of Matter," available on the Internet.

Joe-Joe the Wizard Brews Up Solids, Liquids, and Gases by Eric Braun. Capstone: 2012. (2–3)

Splat!: Wile E Coyote Experiments with States of Matter by Suzanne Slade. Capstone: 2014. (3–6)

The Solid Truth about States of Matter with Max Axiom, Super Scientist by Agnieszka Biskup: Capstone: 2009. (3–4)

LANGUAGE LINK		LEARNING SETTING
Explore:	Vocabulary	Individual
Dig Deeper:	Questions	Partners

Matter and Its Properties

Science Information

Greek philosophers were studying matter as early as 500 BCE. By definition, matter is anything that has mass and takes up space. It is the "stuff" of our world and everything else in the universe. Properties of matter include both physical properties (size, shape, color, and so on) as well as chemical properties (how one kind of matter reacts with other kinds). Aluminum foil, for example, can be described by color, luster, and thickness. It can also be described by how it acts under extreme heat (burns) or when in contact with acids (melts).

We can observe many physical properties of matter with our senses. Many changes that result from chemical properties are directly observable as well, such as the bubbling hydrogen peroxide cleansing a cut.

Science and Engineering Practices: Obtaining, Evaluating, and Communicating Information

Engineers and scientists always want to use the right tool for the right job. Have students conduct research to determine what are the appropriate tools to observe and measure the physical properties of various materials, such as thermometers to measure the heat in a substance or a balance to measure its mass. Students could fold papers to create graphic organizers with which to communicate their information.

EXPLORE
What's the Matter?

Everything matters. Why? Because everything is made of matter. We can describe matter in different ways. Is it hot or cool? Can we see through it? Will it bounce or stretch? These are all properties of matter. Look closely at your pencil. It is made of matter. What are its properties? It is hard and round. It can break. It is very light. Now it's your turn. Select one object from the bag. Place it on your desk. Touch it. Hold it. Smell it. Get the idea? On your paper, list many different properties of your object.

....

Ready? Take

DIG DEEPER
Five Questions

Partners will sit back to back or one partner can have a blindfold lightly attached. One person will pull an object from the bag, and the other person will ask five questions related to properties. "Is it clear?" "Is it made of steel?" "Yes" or "no" answers only. After one partner has hit or missed the name of the object, swap and continue this activity again. Afterward, study your object closely and write two more questions your partner could have asked using different properties.

....

Ready? Take

LANGUAGE LINK		LEARNING SETTING
Explore:	Informative Writing	Individual
Dig Deeper:	Informative Writing	Individual

Mass and Weight

Science Information

For elementary students, the NGSS treat weight and mass as though they are interchangeable. Are they? It depends on where you are in the universe. Mass is a measure of how much matter a thing contains. It is a measurement that would be the same for the object on Earth or on another planet. Consider a typical smartphone. Its mass would be the same on Earth, on the moon, or on Jupiter—about 150 grams. Now weigh a smartphone on Earth, which, in standard units, is about 5.3 ounces. That same smartphone on the moon weighs 0.9 ounce. On Jupiter it weighs 12.4 ounces. Why the difference? The surface gravity of the moon is one-sixth Earth's while the surface gravity of Jupiter is 2.34 times as strong as Earth's. Weight is a measure of the force of gravity on an object. Therefore, because students are weighing their masses on Earth, weight and mass are interchangeable.

Science and Engineering Practices: Using Mathematics and Computational Thinking

Challenge students to find different objects that have the same or nearly the same mass. If balances are unavailable, students might suspend a cup from each end of a ruler or meter stick and balance the midpoint on the back of a chair. Students can place the objects in the cups and then construct comparison statements using drawings and symbols for greater than, less than, and equal.

EXPLORE
Balloon Flight

Two towels are on a chair by the pool. They look alike. But the first towel is dry. The second towel is wet. Do they weigh the same? No. Water adds extra weight. It fills every bit of space between the tiny threads. So the second towel is heavier.

Here is another weight problem. You have three balloons. You blew up one yourself. One is filled with helium, and one is filled with water. Which balloon is heaviest? Explain why it's the heaviest.

Ready? Take

DIG DEEPER
Mass Confusion

Kennedy's mind just wasn't on her upcoming science test. She just couldn't seem to grasp the concept of mass. And so she kept thinking, clicking her pen over and over. Suddenly, she stopped and grabbed a pencil also.

"Hmm, the pen and the pencil are the same size, but the pen is made of steel. I think steel has more molecules inside of it than wood. So the pen has more mass than the pencil."

In this activity, Kennedy compared a pen and a pencil. Now it's your turn. Make a list of other pairs of objects of the same size like a plastic cup and a drinking glass. In each pair circle the one that has more mass. Beneath the list, explain how objects of the same size can differ in mass.

This prompt can further be explored using a balance to check predictions.

Ready? Take

PROMPT SUPPLIES

Mix and Match

Science
Notebook

Colored pencils

All Mixed Up

Science
Notebook

NGSS

2-PS1.A:
Structure and
Properties
of Matter

5-PS1.B: Chemical
Reactions

CCSS

W.K.2, W.1.2,
W.2.2: Support
with Facts

W.3.1, W.4.1,
W.5.1: Support
with Reasons

ADDITIONAL RESOURCES

Search the Internet using the terms
"Mixtures" and "Solutions" to find
such resources as a kitchen mixtures
segment by BrainStewRewind
and "Solutions—Mixing It Up!"

Mix It Up! Solution or Mixture?
by Tracy Nelson Maurer.
Rourke: 2012. (3–4)

Mixtures and Solutions by
Carol Ballard. Heinemann-
Raintree: 2009. (4–5)

LANGUAGE LINK		LEARNING SETTING
Explore:	Informative Writing	Individual
Dig Deeper:	Opinion	Individual

Mixtures

Science Information

Mixtures can be found everywhere. A mixture is a combination
of two or more substances that do not combine chemically but
remain the same individual substances. The substances, once mixed,
can be separated by physical means, although often not very easily.
A simple mixture might be made of equal amounts of pennies,
marbles, and iron washers. The iron washers might be separated
out with a magnet. The marbles could easily be "picked" by hand.
The pennies would remain. Mixtures can be homogenous, or
combinations of two or more substances in which the substances
are mixed evenly, such as air. A heterogeneous mixture is a
combination of two or more substances in which the substances
are not mixed evenly, such as a shaken bottle of oil and water.

Science and Engineering Practices: Engaging in Argument from Evidence

Guide students to make claims backed by evidence concerning
mixtures. They might complete sentences, such as these:

I claim salt water is a mixture because . . .

Muddy water is a mixture because . . .

If I can use a magnet to separate . . . then it is a mixture because . . .

Younger students might use visuals. Give each student one sheet of
acetate and a marker. Have them draw several of one kind of object
on the acetate. Then overlay the acetates on top of each other to
create mixtures. Students might make claims, such as "The bunnies
and flowers are a mixture. They can be separated when the bunnies
hop away and the flowers are left behind."

EXPLORE
Mix and Match

On your paper write these words. They are natural objects.

shell   feather   rock   leaf   pinecone   seed

Next, create a natural mixture. A mixture is a group of different objects. They can be mixed together. But they remain the same. They do not change. Draw a rectangle. This is a large sack. Inside of the sack draw all of your natural objects. Make sure they are all mixed together. Next, draw a line from each object in the sack to its name. Then, answer these questions: "Did the objects in this mixture change into another object? If you ground the seed and pinecone into tiny pieces and mixed together, would it still be a mixture?" Explain your answers.

....

Ready? Take

DIG DEEPER
All Mixed Up

Raj and his twin sister Aisha were having dinner with their aunt. She was preparing one of their favorite dishes: curry over rice with a bowl of mixed nuts and dried fruit. With hungry stomachs they watched her cook the onions and carrots. She then added her spices—curry, cumin, and cinnamon. Slowly, she stirred flour and chicken stock into the pot. This dish was then served over rice. Suddenly, Aisha had an idea. They were having a science quiz the next day, so she decided to test her brother.

"Look carefully at your plate," she instructed him. "Is the curry a mixture? What about the bowl of nuts and fruit?"

These are also your two questions. Consider them carefully and supply your best reasons.

....

Ready? Take

I've Got a Solution	*A Solute to Lemonade*
Two clear cups	Individual packets of lemonade
Sand	
Sugar	Water
Blank note cards	Ice cubes
Water	Cups
Plastic spoons	

NGSS

2-PS1.B: Chemical Reactions

5-PS1.B: Chemical Reactions

CCSS

W.K.2, W.1.2, W.2.2: Support with Facts

W.3.2, W.4.2, W.5.2: Support with Facts

ADDITIONAL RESOURCES

Go into the lab in a "Mixtures and Solutions" video from BrainStewRewind found on the Internet.

This interactive lab provides materials for "Reversible Changes" at http://www.sciencekids.co.nz/gamesactivities/reversiblechanges.html

Mix It Up! Solution or Mixture? by Tracy Nelson Maurer. Rourke: 2012. (3–4)

Mixtures and Solutions by Carol Ballard. Heinemann-Raintree: 2009. (4–5)

LANGUAGE LINK		LEARNING SETTING
Explore:	Informative Writing	Pair
Dig Deeper:	Informative Writing	Individual

Solutions

Science Information

A solution is a special type of mixture called a "homogeneous" mixture. The molecules of all of the substances in a solution are evenly spread out through it. A solution can be a solid dissolved in a liquid, such as sugar in water. The sugar molecules spread out evenly among the water molecules. Solutions can also be gases in liquids (carbonated drinks) or liquids in liquids (food coloring in water). The rate at which a solid dissolves into a liquid can be increased by stirring, heating, or putting the substances under pressure.

Science and Engineering Practices: Using Mathematics and Computational Thinking

In front of the class, mix a small amount of powdered drink mix into a container of water and stir. Then mix an equal amount of soil into another container of water and stir. Allow students to observe the containers for two minutes. Have students create a sequence of diagrams that show what is happening at the microscopic level during that time. Guide students to draw "particles" in each of the substances—water, drink mix, and soil—and show how the particles are spread out in the containers at the beginning, middle, and end of the period of time.

EXPLORE
I've Got a Solution

A solution is a certain kind of mixture. You have two clear cups filled with water. One partner will conduct the first experiment. Pour the sand into the first cup. Slowly stir the sand in the water. Stop. Wait. Look. Where is the sand?

The other person will repeat the same test with sugar. Slowly stir the sugar in the water. Where is the sugar? Use the blank cards. One partner will write "Mixture" at the top. The other partner will write "Solution" at the top. Draw the results of the individual tests. Remember that both of these are mixtures, but only one is a solution. On the back, each of you will answer this question: "How is a solution different from other mixtures?"

DIG DEEPER
A Solute to Lemonade

Unlike other mixtures, materials in a solution are spread out evenly. Try this test. Take the packet of lemonade and pour the contents into the glass of water. Slowly stir. The lemonade crystals will dissolve in the water. In a solution the solute is the substance being dissolved—the crystals. The solvent is the substance causing the crystals to dissolve—water. Think of your kitchen at home. What other items could make a solution? You need two solutions. In a column on your paper, list the solute and the solvent for each. How do you know they formed a solution? Enjoy your lemonade while answering this tangy question.

NGSS : **CCSS**

2-PS1.B: Chemical : W.K.2, W.1.2,
Reactions : W.2.2: Support
: with Facts
5-PS1.A:
Structure and : W.3.3, W.4.3,
Properties : W.5.3: Details
of Matter : and Sequence

ADDITIONAL RESOURCES

Discover interactive activities
at http://www.gamequarium.
org/dir/Gamequarium/Science/
Physical_and_Chemical_Changes/

Explore chemical and physical
changes at https://www.
teachingchannel.org/videos/teaching-
physical-and-chemical-changes

Changing Matter: Understanding
Physical and Chemical Changes
by Tracy Nelson Maurer.
Rourke: 2012. (4–5)

LANGUAGE LINK		LEARNING SETTING
Explore:	Informative Writing	Individual
Dig Deeper:	Narrative Writing	Individual

Physical Change
Science Information

A physical change causes a change to the physical shape of a
substance but does not change the substance into something else.
Also, the amount of matter present before and after a physical
change takes place stays the same. A conversation with students
might go as follows: Have you ever broken anything you really
liked—a glass dolphin or a wooden puzzle? Was it still glass? Was
it still wood? The answer should be "yes" to both questions. These
items underwent a physical change. Think of a small piece of
limestone. You place the piece on a balance and learn that it has a
mass of 50 grams (1.8 ounces). You place the limestone on paper
over a concrete floor. You hit it with a hammer, and it breaks into
several pieces. Are the pieces still limestone? Yes. You carefully place
all of the pieces and the dust onto the balance. Did it read 50 grams
(1.8 ounces)? Yes. What happens if salt is put into water? What is
left after the water evaporates? If you can answer the question "Is it
still what we started with?" with a "yes," then a physical change has
taken place.

Science and Engineering Practices: Planning and Carrying Out Investigations

Give students access to simple materials, such as paper, aluminum
foil, scissors, salt, water, baking soda, vinegar, self-sealing bags,
modeling clay, pieces of balsa wood, and so on. Challenge them
to plan and carry out an investigation that supplies evidence that
physical changes do not change the makeup of a substance. Remind
them to write numbered procedure steps before they begin.

EXPLORE
Time for a Change

Many things can change. A date on a calendar can change. We can also change into warmer clothes, but these are not changes in science. Think about this example. A ball of clay can be changed into many shapes. It's still clay. Sand can be molded into a castle, but it's still sand. In science, these are physical changes. Describe another example of a physical change. Add a drawing to show the object before the change and after the change. Explain why it is a physical change.

DIG DEEPER
Homework Tragedy

Dylan could not believe his luck. His homework fell out of his notebook and landed in a puddle. By the time he realized it was missing, it had been there awhile. He pulled it out. It was soft and mushy. Dylan took it to the hot hand dryer in the boys' bathroom and kept it there until it dried out. It was no longer a wet mess but a piece of paper again. The actual homework was not so lucky. The ink mixed with the water and disappeared from the sheet of paper. He knew he would be in trouble with Mr. Morales, his science teacher.

Suddenly, he had an idea. Maybe he could change his bad luck into good luck. They had been studying physical changes in class. What if he turned this into a science experiment? Maybe all would be forgiven. Write the brief bulleted notes Dylan will need to explain his experiment using the sheet of homework paper as an example. Then write the ending to this story. How does Mr. Morales react?

PROMPT SUPPLIES

Superheroes
Matter

Science
Notebook

Colored pencils

Class Project

Science
Notebook

NGSS

2-PS1.A:
Structure and
Properties
of Matter

5-PS1.A:
Structure and
Properties
of Matter

CCSS

W.K.3, W.1.3,
W.2.3: Imagined
Event

W.3.2.A, ,
W.4.2.A, W.5.2.A:
Supporting
Details

ADDITIONAL RESOURCES

Discover the "States of Matter"
at http://www.chem.purdue.
edu/gchelp/atoms/states.html

Follow the fascinating craft of
glass in the making at http://
www.watchknowlearn.org/
Search: "How is Glass Made"

All About Matter by Mari Schuh.
Capstone: 2012. (PreK–2)

Splat!: Wile E Coyote Experiments
with States of Matter by Suzanne
Slade. Capstone: 2014. (3–6)

The Solid Truth about States of
Matter with Max Axiom, Super
Scientist by Agnieszka Biskup.
Capstone: 2009. (3–4)

LANGUAGE LINK		LEARNING SETTING
Explore:	Narrative Writing	Individual
Dig Deeper:	Informative Writing	Collaboration

States of Matter

Science Information

Matter is found in three familiar states. No, not Florida, Utah, and California! A state is the condition that matter can be found in at a given time. The three common states of matter are solid, liquid, and gas. Scientists recognize some other states of matter, such as plasmas, but they are specialized and rarely naturally occurring.

Water is matter that can be found in three clearly different states at everyday Earth temperatures. Below 0°C (32°F) water is a solid. Its molecules are grouped closely together in an organized "crystalline" pattern. Molecules in a solid can vibrate back and forth, but they do not move around. Above 0°C water is a liquid and can flow to take the shape of the container in which it is being held. The molecules in liquid water are still quite close together, but they do not have a pattern like ice. At 100°C (212°F) water boils. Its molecules have enough energy to leave the liquid and move around in every direction. They fill any container in which they are placed because they spread out so much.

Science and Engineering Practices: Developing and Using Models

Challenge small teams to model the molecular motion of solids, liquids, and gases. They might use water as an example, holding up cards as the temperature changes and counting off degrees (perhaps by 10s) until the next change in state. Older students might add to their models by researching the melting and boiling points of other materials, such as gold or nitrogen.

Superheroes Matter

You are going to draw a comic book. It is about three superheroes. They are called "The Three States of Matter." The first hero is made of liquid like water. The second hero is made of gas like helium in a balloon. The third hero is solid as a rock. What super acts can they do?

Draw three large boxes on your paper. In each box draw a superhero at work. How will they use their super powers? Here are three examples. Liquid State provides water for dying trees. Gas State lifts a bridge and places it over a raging river. Solid State blocks lava from a volcano and saves a town. What will your heroes do?

Class Project

Today, your group will be working on three of the slides for your class presentation on states of matter. Each of you will draw one of three boxes. The first slide will show the gas particles. The second slide will show the liquid particles, and the third will show the solid particles. Under each drawing, write the script you will be using. Explain how the movements and number of particles in each slide reflect the three states of matter. This will take a group effort.

Nature's Magic

Science
Notebook

It's Time for Action

Science
Notebook

NGSS

2-PS1.B: Chemical
Reactions

5-PS1.B: Chemical
Reactions

CCSS

W.K.2, W.1.2,
W.2.2: Support
with Facts

W.3.2, W.4.2,
W.5.2: Support
with Examples

ADDITIONAL RESOURCES

The power of HD and special
lenses capture the beauty
of chemical reactions at
http://beautifulchemistry.
net/reactions.html

Watch as Chemical Bob inflates
a balloon with science at http://
www.instructables.com/id/
Science-Experiment-Inflate-
a-Balloon-with-Vinegar/

*Positive Reaction! A Crash
Course in Science* by Sara L.
Latta. Capstone: 2014. (4–5)

*The Dynamic World of
Chemical Reactions with Max
Axiom* by Agnieszka Biskup.
Capstone: 2011. (3–4)

LANGUAGE LINK		LEARNING SETTING
Explore:	Informative Writing	Individual
Dig Deeper:	Informative Writing	Pair

Chemical Reaction

Science Information

Heating and cooling are physical changes that do not change the
makeup of the substance itself. Solid substances, for example, can
be heated to form a liquid and then cooled to reform a solid. Unlike
a physical change, a chemical change cannot be undone because
the resulting materials are different from the original materials.
A chemical change takes place during a chemical reaction when
substances are mixed, and new substances with different properties
are formed. These changes are not reversible. During a chemical
reaction, the atoms and molecules in the mixed substances break
down and recombine in different ways, often producing invisible
gases. Matter is not created or destroyed, but simply changes form,
and the total mass (weight) of matter (if all could be captured) does
not change.

Science and Engineering Practices: Engaging in Argument from Evidence

Distribute the following materials to teams of students: clear
carbonated soda, two clear plastic cups, a few raisins, baking soda,
and vinegar. Guide them to carry out these steps. (1) Put an equal
amount of soda into one cup and vinegar into another. (2) Gently
stir some baking soda into the vinegar. (3) Place an equal number
of raisins in each cup and observe. (4) Discuss with teammates
the chemical reactions observed. (5) Create a diagram with brief
captions that cite evidence to explain the reactions.

EXPLORE
Nature's Magic

In a chemical reaction, at least one lasting change takes place. Mix sugar, flour, water, and salt. Bake it in the oven. What happens? It changes into bread. That is a chemical reaction. The loaf of bread can't change back into sugar, flour, water, and salt. What do these two things have in common: a leaf turning red in the fall and a boiled egg? Did you say chemical reactions? That's right! The leaf won't turn green again, and the egg won't turn back into a raw egg. Think of another example of a chemical reaction. Draw a before and after picture. Explain what happens.

DIG DEEPER
It's Time for Action

In a chemical reaction, two substances combine to form a new substance. It's like the fizzing that occurs when combining vinegar and baking soda. It's the burst of color when fireworks explode. Let's think of other ways to describe a chemical reaction. What two other substances could be combined to make a new substance? What if a tomato reacted with a cucumber? You would get a cucumator. With a partner, consider other possible combinations. What can you produce from two other substances? Write a description of the two objects and the reaction that occurred. Provide an illustration.

Science
Notebook

Science
Notebook

NGSS

K-PS2.A: Forces
and Motion

K-PS3.C:
Relationship
Between Energy
and Forces

3-PS2.A: Forces
and Motion

CCSS

W.K.2, W.1.2,
W.2.2: Support
with Facts

W.3.2, W.4.2,
W.5.2: Support
with Details

ADDITIONAL RESOURCES

Discover more about "Force
and Motion" with Bill Nye,
available on the Internet.

*A Crash Course in Forces and Motion
with Max Axiom, Super Scientist* by
Emily Sohn. Capstone: 2007. (3–4)

*DO-4U the Robot Experiences
Forces and Motion* by Mark
Weakland. Capstone: 2012. (2–3)

*Zombies and Force and
Motion* by Mark Weakland.
Capstone: 2011. (3–4)

LANGUAGE LINK		LEARNING SETTING
Explore:	Informative Writing	Individual
Dig Deeper:	Informative Writing	Individual

Force

Science Information

Forces are pushes and pulls used to do work, or make changes. On
a playground, forces applied by muscles slow, speed up, or change
the direction of playground equipment. The force of gravity pulls on
the samaras of maple tree seeds as they helicopter their way down
to the ground. The buoyant force of water pushes up a boat made
of metal foil with a rock as a passenger. The force of friction causes
one's palms to warm as hands are rubbed together. A marble sitting
on a table doesn't move though the forces of gravity and friction
act on it. Most people would be unable to resist reaching out with
their fingers to supply an unbalanced force to cause the marble to
roll off the table to create a racket.

Science and Engineering Practices: Engaging in Argument from Evidence

In small groups, have students discuss scenarios of a force being
applied during a school activity. Examples include writing out a
math problem, manipulating the lunch tray through the cafeteria
line, or sharpening a pencil. The group could then act out the
scenario, with each member of the team demonstrating the
pushes and pulls involved and citing evidence as to why they are
applications of force.

EXPLORE
Snow Day

Victor was so excited. During the night a thick blanket of snow covered the town. Quickly, Victor grabbed his sled and headed for Runaway Hill. He pulled and grunted, but finally reached the top. Here, others were gathered. Each person took turns pushing each other over the top of the hill. Zoom! Down they would fly, but then it was time for the long walk back to the top. Time to pull that sled again.

Push and pull are forces. Think of another fun activity, one that includes both forces. Draw two pictures, one with a push and the other a pull. Under each picture, explain the force being used in the activity.

....

Ready? Take

DIG DEEPER
Target Practice

Marina has won many awards for archery. You have been given the job of filming her for an upcoming television program. Zoom in for some tight shots. First, she places her feet shoulder-width apart with her left side facing the target. She pulls an arrow from her quiver, or case for holding arrows. Next, she points the bow and arrow toward the ground as she lays the arrow against the bow. She then notches the arrow, or inserts the string into the back of the arrow. In one motion, she raises the bow, takes aim at her target, and pulls back on the arrow. Zing! The arrow is released. It flies straight toward the target. Bull's-eye! Now the real work begins for you. Many of Marina's actions demonstrate the use of force (pushing or pulling). Create still shots (pictures) of at least three actions. Beneath each picture, write a caption that explains the force being used. These will be used to promote the film *Force and Archery*.

....

Ready? Take

Get Moving!

Science
Notebook

Motion Sickness

Science
Notebook

NGSS

K-PS2.A: Forces
and Motion

K-PS3.C:
Relationship
Between Energy
and Forces

3-PS2.A: Forces
and Motion

CCSS

L.K.5.A, L.1.5.A,
L.2.5.A: Sorting

W.3.2.B, W.4.2.B,
W.5.2.B: Support
with Details

ADDITIONAL RESOURCES

"The Motion Song" will turn
things around for young viewers at
http://www.learninggamesforkids.
com/science-games/science-
songs/motion-song-2.html

Get into the circus act at
http://www.pbs.org/ Search:
"Newton's Laws of Motion"

Making Things Move by Siam Smith.
Heinemann-Raintree: 2009. (PreK–1)

*Zombies and Force and
Motion* by Mark Weakland.
Capstone: 2011. (3–4)

LANGUAGE LINK		LEARNING SETTING
Explore:	Vocabulary	Individual
Dig Deeper:	Informative Writing	Team

Motion

Science Information

Is there motion when an object is sitting still? What about at the molecular level? An object is in motion when it is moving. An object is moving when it is changing position. For something to be set in motion, a force (push or pull) must act on it. Stronger pushes or pulls can speed up or slow down the motion of an object. Objects in motion can have a set distance they travel, speed (how long it takes to travel a given distance), velocity (speed in a given direction), and acceleration (a change in velocity).

Science and Engineering Practices: Analyzing and Interpreting Data

Have students find pictures of inanimate objects in motion and discuss with small groups about how they know motion is occurring. They should also try to identify the applied force that resulted in the motion. For example, students might say that wind or moving air is turning the blades of a windmill. They can tell the blades are turning because the blades are blurred.

Get Moving!

It's time to get moving! Stand up. Keep one arm's length apart from your neighbors. Let's begin. Raise your arms. Stretch them toward the ceiling. Now wave your arms in the air. Put them back down. Lean to the left. Now lean to the right. March up and down in one place. Now stop! What have you done? You've been in motion. Motion is movement. It is a change in position. And that's what you did. What else can be put in motion? Place your pencil on the desk or table. Now set it in motion. Gently spin it around. Motion is everywhere. Draw three more examples of objects in motion. Under each picture write the motion. Here are more examples: swimming, jumping, a kite flying in the sky. Put your thinking wheels in motion.

Motion Sickness

"Stop!" Stefan begged. "I want off this thing!"

Too bad, Stefan. You can't stop a roller coaster in mid-motion. You will have to wait until it stops. Many people suffer from motion sickness. This often happens on amusement park rides, boats, and airplanes—too much rolling, tumbling, and twisting. That's why some people have to face the front when riding a bus or train. Their eyes connect what is being seen with what is being felt. And right now, Stefan feels very sick.

Stefan and others like him need your team to design a different amusement ride—one that will not cause many changes in motion. Perhaps it could go underwater. Make notes on the design that explain each change in motion.

Racetrack

Science
Notebook

Bull's-Eye

Science
Notebook

NGSS

K-PS2.A: Forces
and Motion

3-PS2.A: Forces
and Motion

CCSS

W.K.1, W.1.1,
W.2.1: Support
with Reasons

W.3.1.B, W.4.1.B,
W.5.1.B: Support
with Reasons

ADDITIONAL RESOURCES

The difference between speed
and velocity is musically explained
at http://watchknowlearn.org/
Search: "Speed and Velocity Song"

Speed and Acceleration by
Barbara A. Somervill. Heinemann-
Raintree: 2010. (3–6)

The Science of Speed, a four-book set,
by Suzanne Slade, Lori Hile, Karen
Latchana Kenney, Marcia Amidon
Lusted. Capstone: 2014. (5–9)

LANGUAGE LINK		LEARNING SETTING
Explore:	Opinion	Individual
Dig Deeper:	Opinion	Individual

Speed and Velocity

Science Information

At these grade levels, the NGSS begin to build background for the
ideas of speed and velocity even though the terms are not included.
Recall the distance–time formula: Distance = Rate x Time. In a word
problem format, it might look like this: If Salia peddles her bicycle
at 10 mph for 2 hours, how far will she travel? 20 miles. Right? If we
were to solve the problem for rate, we would have Rate = Distance
÷ Time. Rate = 20 miles ÷ 2 hours. The answer? 10 mph. But what
is 10 mph? Based on the formula, the ready answer is Rate, or
distance divided by time, which is the same as "speed." Surprised?
Speed is the measure of how fast something is moving. Back to
Salia: If Salia peddles her bicycle at 10 mph west on Martin Luther
King Boulevard for 2 hours, how far will she travel? Does the "west"
change things? It most certainly does. Speed in a specific direction
is velocity. Without the direction, Salia could have been headed
anywhere from her starting point.

Science and Engineering Practices: Developing and Using Models

Students might use manipulatives to demonstrate the difference
between speed and velocity. Students should come quickly to the
conclusion that, however they move their manipulatives, they are
always moving them in a given direction that could be identified
with a compass. Younger students might practice measuring various
long distances with meter sticks, such as down the hallway, and use
a stopwatch to time how long it takes to walk a given distance. That
will tell them their speed, or steps per second (or steps per minute).

EXPLORE
Racetrack

Mrs. Weeks placed a board on a box. The board slanted to the floor. Down the hallway, she placed another board. This one ran across the hall from wall to wall. What was she doing? The first board was the start of the car race. The second board would stop the cars. Her students had made their own race cars. Which car was the fastest?

She used a stopwatch and recorded the time for each car. Some cars were in rectangle shapes. Some were wedge shaped. Also, some cars had plastic wheels, and some had wood wheels. What does your car look like? Draw your car and provide a description. Explain why this car would have the fastest time.

....

DIG DEEPER
Bull's-Eye

"That's strange. We missed again," Ally frowned. "What is wrong with our device?" She placed another rubber ball into a small cup, pulled back the rubber band, and released it. The ball missed the target again. "It needs more speed."

"Don't you mean velocity?" Claire answered. "Running in a track meet, now that takes speed. A quarterback throwing a football to a receiver? That's accuracy, and that means velocity. It's how fast you're going in a certain direction. And that's what we need—to go in the direction of the target."

Provide another example. When is speed more important than velocity? Why? Provide another example. When is velocity more important than speed? Why?

....

PROMPT SUPPLIES

Speed Racer	*Biker Fashion Design*
Science Notebook	Science Notebook
	Colored pencils

NGSS

K-PS2.A: Forces and Motion

3-PS2.A: Forces and Motion

CCSS

W.K.2, W.1.2, W.2.2: Support with Facts

W.3.2, W.4.2, W.5.2: Support with Facts

ADDITIONAL RESOURCES

Bill Nye the Science Guy takes on "Friction," available on the Internet.

Predict the right surface for skateboarding at http://www.learninggamesforkids.com/motion-games/friction-ramp.html

DO-4U the Robot Experiences Forces and Motion by Mark Weakland. Capstone: 2012. (2–3)

Sports by Chris Oxlade. Capstone: 2012. (2–4)

LANGUAGE LINK		LEARNING SETTING
Explore:	Informative Writing	Individual
Dig Deeper:	Informative Writing	Individual

Friction

Science Information

Friction is a force that acts on objects touching one another. As the surface of one object moves across the surface of another, force is exerted. Between very textured or rough surfaces, this force is much greater than between smooth surfaces like that of a bowling ball and the alley. Substances, such as water and oil, can reduce the force of friction even more.

Yet, the key is the total force on an object. It is possible that several forces might be acting on an object like a huge rock on top of a hill. You could be pushing it while gravity is pulling it, but because of the force of friction, the rock stays in place.

Science and Engineering Practices: Engaging in Argument from Evidence

Students might use magnifying glasses to examine the palms of their hands. They could first create a drawing that shows what happens when they rub their dry hands together. Then they could create a drawing showing how covering their hands with soap fills the ridges. Have them cite evidence why soap reduces friction and causes their hands to be slippery.

EXPLORE
Speed Racer

Will is ready to have fun with his go-kart. He wants more speed. Gravity pulls it down the hill. But the wheels on Will's go-kart do not turn very quickly. They slowly roll down the grassy hill. The grass and the wheels rub against each other. This causes friction. Friction is a force. It can slow down a moving object.

Will wants less friction. He does not want to go slow. He looks at the wooden wheels. They are bumpy along the edges. This must be slowing down the go-kart. He looks at the track on the hill. The grass is long.

Name three ways Will can reduce friction. Use complete sentences.

DIG DEEPER
Biker Fashion Design

Each morning before school, Bailey and Kadarius hop on their bicycles and ride for an hour. They are training for a bike race. Along with getting themselves in physical shape, they are also getting their bikes in shape. Their goal is to reduce as much friction, or resistance, as possible. Their tires are light and smooth. The gears and all moving parts are oiled well. But they need to do more to overcome friction. The more surface area exposed to the wind, the more friction it causes. They need specially designed riding helmets and clothes to cut smoothly through the wind as they ride. This is your task. Design very special clothing, helmets, and/or bicycles for one of these two competitors. Remember the goal: Reduce friction! Beneath the drawing, explain how each part will reduce friction.

NGSS : **CCSS**

K-PS2.A: Forces : W.K.2.,W.1.2,
and Motion : W.2.2: Support
: with Examples
3-PS2.B: Types :
of Interactions : W.3.2.B, W.4.2.B,
: W.5.2.B: Support
: with Examples

ADDITIONAL RESOURCES

Watch this animated cartoon about magnets at http://dev. hooplakidz.com/showcase-video?play=119&sq=18

The National Geographic website explores magnets at two videos found at http://www.nationalgeographic. com Search: "magnets"

Bill Nye the Science Guy explores magnetism in the video "Magnetism," available on the Internet.

Magnets in the Real World by Chris Eboch. Abdo Publishing: 2013. (4–5)

Magnets Push, Magnets Pull by Mark Weakland. Capstone: 2011. (K–2)

The Attractive Story of Magnetism with Max Axiom, Super Scientist by Andrea Gianopoulos. Capstone: 2008. (3–4)

LANGUAGE LINK		LEARNING SETTING
Explore:	Informative Writing	Individual
Dig Deeper:	Informative Writing	Individual

Magnets

Science Information

A magnet is a material that creates a magnetic field, which extends outward from the material itself. Because of the magnetic field, magnets apply a force at a distance—a distance that varies with the magnet's strength. Magnets attract things that are made of iron, nickel, and cobalt. Materials like wood, plastic, and cloth are not magnetic.

All magnets have two poles where the attractive forces of the magnet are strongest. If a common bar magnet is suspended from a string, it will freely rotate to align itself to Earth's magnetic field. One pole, the north seeking, will point toward Earth's North Pole. The other, the south-seeking pole, points toward Earth's South Pole—thus N and S. Disc magnets have poles as well. They may not be labeled N and S, but the opposite poles attract and the like ones repel, so a letter or symbol could be assigned to them if needed.

Science and Engineering Practices: Using Mathematics and Computational Thinking

Allow students to explore the distance across which the magnetic force can act and how that varies among magnets of the same kind and shape and those of different shapes. They might use paper clips as nonstandard units to collect and graph data. Students might also determine the relative strengths of magnets by measuring the distance at which two magnets repel each other.

EXPLORE
Magnets at Work

Magnets have a north pole and a south pole. Opposite ends of magnets attract each other (north to south). The same ends repel each other (north to north). Their ability to attract metal objects makes them an important tool. They are used in computer screens, telephones, vending machines, and compasses. In your home, a magnet keeps the refrigerator door closed. How could you use a magnet? It could pick up your toys. At school it could sort metal cans from the trash. These cans could then be recycled. Now it's your turn. How could a magnet be a useful tool at home and at school?

Ready? Take

DIG DEEPER
Lost!

Sophia's class was enjoying a fun trip to Landmark Park. The students eagerly followed its paths. Sophia and her friend Caroline stopped to watch turtles sunning on a log. Suddenly, Sophia looked up.

"Where did everyone go?" she asked. "Which way is the bus?"

Caroline pulled a compass from her pocket. "No worries. The magnet in this compass will show us the way," she assured her friend.

A compass isn't the only way a magnet can be used. Describe two other ways magnets could be used at the park to help keep animals and visitors safe. For each example, explain how each magnet accomplished the task.

Ready? Take

NGSS | **CCSS**

K-PS3.C: | W.K.3, W.1.3,
Relationship | W.2.3: Imagined
Between Energy | Event
and Forces |
 | W.3.2.B, W.4.2.B,
4-PS3.A: | W.5.2.B: Support
Definitions of | with Examples
Energy |

4-PS3.C:
Relationship
Between Energy
and Forces

ADDITIONAL RESOURCES

NOVA presents "Energy Defined" at
NOVA Education link www.pbs.org

Young viewers will get energized
with the "Energy Song" at the
Learning Games for Kids website.

The potential for laughter
abounds in "Potential Energy:
Wile E Coyote & Roadrunner"
at WatchKnowLearn website.

Aliens and Energy by Agnieszka
Biskup. Capstone: 2011. (3–4)

The Power of Energy by Rebecca
Weber. Capstone: 2011. (PreK–1)

LANGUAGE LINK		LEARNING SETTING
Explore:	Narrative Writing	Individual
Dig Deeper:	Informative Writing	Individual

Energy
Science Information

Ever feel low on energy? Energy is the ability to do work (cause motion) or cause change. The energy of a moving rubber ball can move toys out of its path. If the ball is larger or rolling at a faster speed, it will have more energy and knock more toys out of the way. If the ball is smaller or rolling at a slower speed, it will have less energy and knock fewer toys out of the way. Food eaten by animals allows them to move, do work, and grow because it transfers energy from the sun to the cells of the body. Energy is classified as potential (stored energy) and kinetic (energy of motion) and includes chemical, mechanical, nuclear, gravitational, radiant, thermal, motion, and electrical energy.

Science and Engineering Practices: Using Mathematics and Computational Thinking

Challenge students to develop flowcharts that show the movement or transfer of energy from its original source (the sun) to students' actions on the playground (sun → grass → cow → human → kicked soccer ball), a car's movement (sun → ancient plants → ancient animals → gasoline → car's moving wheels), or a book's placement on a high shelf (sun → grass → cow → human → upstretched arm → stored energy in book).

Nut-ercized!

The squirrel stared at the two nuts on the ground. They would be so tasty this winter. But there was a problem. Too many people were in the park. So the squirrel waited. It sat quietly. Finally, everyone left. The squirrel ran to the nuts. It popped them into its cheeks.

Now the squirrel is tired. It used so much energy running and gathering nuts. Energy is the ability to do work. At first, the squirrel did not use much energy. It just sat and waited. Then, the squirrel did a lot of work! It used so much energy! Draw a picture of a park. There is so much energy being used here. Who or what is doing work? Draw at least two other scenes showing energy in the park. Label each example of energy being used—like the squirrel running and gathering the nuts. Explain the energy being used.

....

Ready? Take

Get Energized!

Energy is the ability to do work. Megan has the ability to work. She's just lying on the grass looking at the blueberries she is supposed to pick. But there's so many, she's thinking. It's going to take a lot of work to pick them all. Megan has the potential, or the ability, to get the work done, but not the right motivation. Suddenly, she sees her father's car turning in the driveway. Up she hops, grabs her bucket, and starts picking the ripe berries. Now, she's showing kinetic energy, or energy in motion. All around Megan's home are more examples of kinetic and potential energy. Describe at least two of each.

....

Ready? Take

Electricity Rap

Science Notebook

Forgotten Powers

Science Notebook

NGSS

2-PS1.A: Structure and Properties of Matter

4-PS3.B: Conservation of Energy

CCSS

L.K.5.A, L.1.5.A, L.2.5.A: Categories

W.3.3, W.4.3, W.5.3: Imagined Event and Energy Transfer

ADDITIONAL RESOURCES

Electricity bakes more than a cake. It can give life to Frankenstein. Discover the process at "It's Alive!!!" at http://pbskids.org/

Create your own electricity at "Static Electricity: Snap, Crackle, Jump" at http://www.pbslearningmedia.org

Electricity by Louise Spilsbury and Richard Spilsbury. Heinemann-Raintree: 2013. (4–6)

The Boy Who Harnessed the Wind by William Kamkwamba. Dial Books for Young Readers: 2009. (1–3)

Zombies and Electricity by Mark Weakland. Capstone: 2013. (3–9)

LANGUAGE LINK		LEARNING SETTING
Explore:	Vocabulary	Collaborative
Dig Deeper:	Narrative Writing	Individual

Electricity

Science Information

Electricity, or flowing electric current, is the energy that is moved from place to place in the wires we see everywhere. What energy moves in the electric current? Electric energy is derived from the presence of charged particles in atoms. The charged particles in an atom are electrons (negative) and protons (positive). When electrons move from one atom to another (as in a wire), an electric current is created. Electrons (and electricity) move well through materials that have loosely held electrons. Materials made of atoms with loosely held electrons, such as many metals, are conductors.

Science and Engineering Practices: Asking Questions and Defining Problems

To raise the awareness of young students to the pervasiveness of electricity, have small groups of students talk about the items they use that are powered by electricity. Then, help students identify the problem solved by using each item, such as fixing toast for breakfast or keeping warm with an electric blanket. Challenge students to imagine how the task would be accomplished without the use of electricity.

Electricity Rap

Flip a switch, and a light comes on. Mash a button, and music plays. Welcome to the world of electricity. Electricity is a flow of energy. It isn't like the sun's energy. The sun's energy is natural. You can't turn the sun's energy off or on. What else uses electricity?

A refrigerator keeps food cold. How?

It's electric!

The clock hands move 'round and 'round keeping time. How?

It's electric!

Keep this electric rap song going. Add three more actions to the above list. End each sentence with the question "How?"

Don't forget to add the words "It's electric!"

 *Ready? Take* **5!**

Forgotten Powers

Many names are associated with electrical discoveries. There's Michael Faraday and his electric motor. There's also Ben Franklin whose lightning rod sent a powerful bolt of electricity to the ground, preventing wooden structures of his day from catching fire. Of course, there's the popular Thomas Edison and his lightbulb. But history has forgotten your (imaginary) uncle and his electrical contribution. Create an encyclopedia entry for this man and describe the electrical discovery, how he discovered it, and its purpose.

 *Ready? Take* **5!**

PROMPT SUPPLIES

Pancakes with Butter

Science Notebook

Booster's Winter Home

Science Notebook

NGSS

2-PS1.A: Structure and Properties of Matter

4-PS3.A: Definitions of Energy

CCSS

W.K.2, W.1.2, W.2.2: Support with Facts

W.3.2, W.4.2, W.5.2: Support with Details

ADDITIONAL RESOURCES

Young scientists are "Testing Insulators: Ice Cube in a Box" at http://www.pbslearningmedia.org

"Circuits & Conductors" and "Heat Transfer," can be found at the Science Kids website.

Go "Exploring Conductivity: Kid Circuits" at http://www.pbslearningmedia.org

Get rocking with the music video "Conduction, Radiation, Convection Song" by Untamed Science, available on the Internet.

Conductors and Insulators by Chris Oxlade. Capstone: 2012. (2–4)

Electricity All Around by Barbara Alpert. Capstone: 2011. (K–1)

LANGUAGE LINK		LEARNING SETTING
Explore:	Informative Writing	Individual
Dig Deeper:	Informative Writing	Collaboration

Conductors and Insulators

Science Information

Different properties are best suited for different purposes. Often properties are opposite to each other. A conductor is a material that energy can easily move through. Metals are usually good conductors. Copper, platinum, silver, gold, and aluminum are materials through which electricity and heat can move easily. Water and trees are also good conductors of electricity. An insulator is a material that energy cannot move through easily, nor does it transfer an electric charge easily. Wood, rubber, and plastic are all good insulators. Consider how a modern frying pan with a plastic handle utilizes both conductors and insulators to serve its purpose.

Science and Engineering Practices: Obtaining, Evaluating, and Communicating Information

Show students pictures of household items and objects they come in contact with, such as cookware, electrical devices, and space heaters. Challenge them to identify the parts that would keep the object cool to the touch or that might make it warm for a specific purpose, such as cooking food.

Pancakes with Butter

Yum! It's pancake day. Addie loves to help her dad make pancakes.

"Watch out!" he warns her. "Don't get too close to the griddle."

Addie minds her dad. Meanwhile, she butters the pancakes with a small butter knife.

Uh-oh! She lays the knife down. It touches the griddle. She picks it up again.

"Ouch!" she cries. The griddle is made of metal. The butter knife is made of metal. The metal griddle conducted its heat to the metal knife. This made the knife hot. Addie needs some safety advice for the kitchen. Write her a note. Use the word "conduct" in your answer.

Booster's Winter Home

Brrr! It is so cold outside. You need to turn up the heat and snuggle under a thick blanket. Unfortunately, Booster, a Great Dane, cannot come inside. How can he stay warm in his outdoor pen? As a team, use your knowledge of conductors and insulators. Items, such as aluminum, iron, concrete, glass, water, and silver will conduct, or move heat, to a cooler object. Devise a way for these items to be heated without electricity. You will need insulators to prevent the heat from escaping. Design a warm winter home for Booster. Each item needs to produce the desired effect. Put on your thinking caps as you conduct this project. Then, explain this plan.

PROMPT SUPPLIES

Hot Stuff

Science
Notebook

Fired Up

Science
Notebook

NGSS

K-PS3.B:
Conservation
of Energy and
Energy Transfer

4-PS3.B:
Conservation
of Energy and
Energy Transfer

CCSS

W.K.2, W.1.2,
W.2.2: Support
with Examples/
Facts

W.3.3, W.4.3,
W.5.3: Imagined
Event

ADDITIONAL RESOURCES

The Learning Games for Kids
website provides a variety of
resources, including the "Heat
Energy Song" at http://www.
learninggamesforkids.com/heat-
energy-games/heat-energy-song.html

Bill Nye the Science Guy takes
some "Heat" in this video,
available on the Internet.

The National Geographic website
presents "Energy 101: Geothermal
Heat Pumps" at http://www.
learninggamesforkids.com/heat-
energy-games/heat-energy-song.html

*From Crude Oil to Fast Food Snacks:
An Energy Journey Through the
World of Heat* by Ian Graham.
Heinemann-Raintree: 2015. (3–6)

Investigating Heat (Searchlight Books)
by Sally M. Walker. Lerner: 2012. (2–5)

LANGUAGE LINK		LEARNING SETTING
Explore:	Informative Writing	Individual
Dig Deeper:	Narrative Writing	Individual

Heat

Science Information

Heat is the flow of energy from a warmer object to a cooler object.
When the energy (light) of the sun shines on the surface of the
Earth, Earth is warmed. When energy (light) is added to Earth,
Earth's temperature increases. If an ice cube were placed on the sun-
warmed Earth, heat energy would move from Earth to the ice cube.
Heat and motion are related. As the ice cube melts, the molecules
that comprise it begin to move faster, releasing heat. Objects
moving in contact with each other release heat through friction
because of conservation of energy. The energy of motion eventually
changes to heat as objects slow and stop. In the NGSS at the K–5
grade levels, the term "heat" may be used interchangeably with the
term "thermal energy."

Science and Engineering Practices: Analyzing and Interpreting Data

Project or draw a graph like the one below. Add drawings (or have
students do so) that would show the appearance of a container
holding water for each segment of the graph. Have students make
claims about the role of heat in water changing from solid ice to
the gas water vapor based on the data in the graph and about why
the graph flattens out in the "ice and water" and "water and steam"
areas. Guide younger students to connect the graph line to the axes
and discuss what the graph shows.

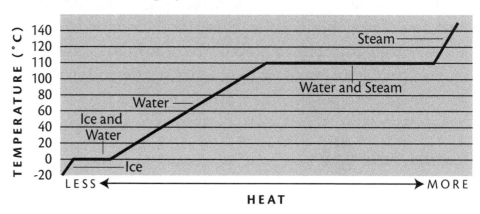

EXPLORE
Hot Stuff

Your family loves a snowy day. There are snowballs to throw, and snowmen to build. There are hills to sled. But you are getting very, very cold. A sudden thought hits you. Motion releases heat. You need more motion! What can you do? Draw or write two different solutions to this problem. Then explain how shivering helps to warm our bodies.

Ready? Take

DIG DEEPER
Fired Up

Many people enjoy a warm campfire in the fall of the year. Are you a little cool? Imagine you are outdoors beside a roaring fire. Stand close to the open flames. Hold up your hands. The heat is thermal energy. This energy moves from the fire to your hands. Hungry? Grab a wire coat hanger and attach a marshmallow to the end. Hold it close to the fire. Energy from the warmer object (the coat hanger) is transferred to the cooler object (your hand). Ouch! Be careful around a fire. Describe another scene where heat, or thermal energy, is transferred from one object to another. Explain the heat transfer in steps—what happens first, next, and last.

Ready? Take

NGSS

K-PS3.B: Conservation of Energy and Energy Transfer

4-PS3.A: Definitions of Energy

CCSS

W.K.1, W.1.1, W.2.1: Support with Reasons

W.3.3, W.4.3, W.5.3: Imagined Event

ADDITIONAL RESOURCES

Convert temperature and determine the wind chill and index at http://www.weatherwizkids.com/weather-temperature.htm.

Listen and follow along with the lyrics at "The Thermometer Song" (song for kids about temperature) found on the Internet.

All About Temperature by Alison Auch. Capstone: 2011. (PreK–1)

Temperature by Casey Rand. Capstone: 2011. (3–6)

LANGUAGE LINK		LEARNING SETTING
Explore:	Opinion	Individual
Dig Deeper:	Narrative	Individual

Temperature

Science Information

While our first thought about "temperature" is to think about how hot something is, it's time to delve a bit deeper. Temperature is a measure of the heat, or thermal energy, something possesses. The more thermal energy something has, the more its atoms and molecules move around. This action transfers energy to the bulb of a thermometer, causing that liquid (mercury or alcohol colored red) to warm as well. So the liquid expands because the atoms or molecules in it move farther apart. Therefore, the liquid in the tube rises. Similarly, a microwave causes the molecules in the food that is being heated to move more rapidly at the same time and thus the food warms.

Science and Engineering Practices: Developing and Using Models

Students might make a model of a thermometer. They could construct one using a tall, narrow plastic bottle, a straw, water, rubbing alcohol, food coloring, and clay. They would fill the bottle about one-fourth full of equal parts alcohol and water and add a few drops of food coloring. They would insert the straw and seal the opening of the bottle with clay. As students move their models to warmer areas or cooler areas, they will see the liquid move up and down in the straw. Students should make claims about how their models explain what happens when the thermometer comes in contact with something that is cooler or hotter.

What Should I Wear?

Hot cold is it? We could step outside and feel the air. But there is another way. Read a thermometer. A thermometer is a science tool. It measures heat in the air using degrees. The number of degrees is the temperature. There is little heat in the air at 32°F (0°C). It snows at that temperature. But it can go even lower! There is a lot of heat in the air at 80°F (27°C). But it can go higher!

What is your favorite temperature? Write this temperature at the top of your paper. Then, draw yourself. Be sure to wear the right clothes. Include in the drawing one activity you enjoy in this temperature. Below the drawing, answer this question: "Why is this your favorite temperature?"

....

Weather Alert

Temperature measures the amount of heat in the air. The higher the temperature, the more heat is in the air. The National Weather Service needs to issue a Heat Advisory for your area. Warnings are issued for unusually hot weather that lasts for several days in a row. A Caution warning is issued for temperatures 80°F (27°C) and above and an Extreme Caution Warning for temperatures at 90°F (32°C). A Danger Alert is the next level. Temperatures of 126°F (52°C) and above would rate an Extreme Danger Alert. Write a heat advisory for local media (television, radio, newspaper). Provide the advisory level and a reason for the alert. Also include steps people can take to protect themselves against the heat.

....

NGSS

1-PS4.A: Wave
Properties

4-PS3.A:
Definitions
of Energy

CCSS

W.K.2, W.1.2,
W.2.2: Support
with Examples

W.3.2, W.4.2,
W.5.2: Support
with Examples

ADDITIONAL RESOURCES

Watch these experiments with sound at http://www.pbslearningmedia.org Search: "sound and solids"

Younger students will grasp the sounds of vibrations at http://www.pbslearningmedia.org Search: "understanding vibration and pitch"

Sing along with the "Vibration Song Video" at http://www.learninggamesforkids.com/science_songs/vibration-science-song.html

Experiments with Sound by Isabel Thomas: Heinemann-Raintree: 2015. (2–4)

Sound and Hearing by Catherine Vietch. Heinemann-Raintree: 2009. (PreK–1)

LANGUAGE LINK		LEARNING SETTING
Explore:	Informative Writing	Individual
Dig Deeper:	Informative Writing	Individual

Vibrations

Science Information

Cell phone. Desk with a printer sitting on it. Atoms. Electric toothbrush. A house close to the railroad tracks. Speakers connected to an audio system. Plates and glasses in a cabinet during an earthquake. What do these things have in common? They are all objects that can vibrate. Objects that are vibrating move back and forth rapidly, indicating how much energy is moving through them. Remember the lore about the opera singer and the wine glass? She produces a very loud sound (tone) that produces vibrations with wavelengths that match those that could cause the wineglass to vibrate itself to pieces. To see a demonstration conducted at Harvard University, use an Internet keyword search "Harvard shattering wineglass."

Science and Engineering Practices: Using Mathematics and Computational Thinking

Give students a collection of objects with which they can produce vibrations, such as plastic rulers, rubber bands, string, plastic bowls with lids, and so on. Challenge them to devise a way to give each one the same amount of energy to produce a vibration in it. Have them rank the objects according to how much of the mechanical energy they supplied was converted to sound energy. Students might use a decibel meter (available as a smart phone app) or their own qualitative observations to rank the objects.

Good Vibrations

Did you hear that? It sounds like a vibration! A what? A VIBRATION! Sorry, I didn't mean to shout. Vibrations are tiny movements. They go back and forth very quickly. They create the sounds you hear. You can also feel a vibration. Very quietly begin humming. Place your hand to your throat. Feel the vibrations? Vibrations can travel through air and water. A whale calls its pod. The vibrations move through the water, and the pod hears the sound. Imagine you are in the deep ocean. List two sounds you might hear. What caused the vibrations? Draw a picture to go with your sounds.

Sounds Like

Suddenly, a dog's ears perk up. Did you hear anything? Possibly not since dogs can hear sounds undetected by humans. Many animals and insects have keen sense organs that can detect lifesaving vibrations. It's good to know when a predator is coming your way. Imagine having sound coming at you at 50,000 vibrations per second. But that's approximately how sharp a dog's hearing is with ranges as high as 100,000 per second. Humans average only 10,000 vibrations per second. The faster the vibrations the higher the sound. That's why dogs can hear very high-pitched sounds.

Think of two sounds. Name each sound. Based on the above information, do you think the sound's vibrations are fast or slow? Explain why.

PROMPT SUPPLIES

Wave Power	*Riding the Waves*
Science Notebook	Science Notebook

NGSS

1-PS4.A: Wave Properties

4-PS4.A: Wave Properties

CCSS

W.K.2, W.1.2, W.2.2: Support with Facts

W.3.3, W.4.3, W.5.3: Sequence of Events

ADDITIONAL RESOURCES

Music and color come together as light waves are captured using highly advanced technology in "Unbelievable Trillion Frames Per Second Camera Captures Light in Motion" found on the Internet.

Bill Nye the Science Guy's "Baby I Love Your Wave," found on the Internet, parodies the Peter Frampton tune.

Adventures in Sound with Max Axiom, Super Scientist by Emily Sohn. Capstone: 2007. (3–4)

From Crashing Waves to Music Download: An Energy Journey Through the World of Sound by Andrew Solway. Heinemann-Raintree: 2015. (3–6)

Light and Sound by Wendy Meshbesher and Eve Hartman. Heinemann-Raintree: 2010. (4)

LANGUAGE LINK		LEARNING SETTING
Explore:	Informative Writing	Individual
Dig Deeper:	Narrative Writing	Individual

Waves

Science Information

A wave is a disturbance that transfers energy. As a wave passes through matter, the matter moves up and down or side to side. But the matter doesn't travel over a distance. For example, when a water wave passes under a buoy, the buoy moves up and down. But it stays in the same location. The energy carried by the wave, however, moves on to bob the next buoy or boat. If the wave carries a lot of energy, the buoy bobs higher than if the wave carries less energy.

Some waves, called mechanical waves, can travel only through matter—solid, liquid, or gas. Seismic or earthquake waves carry energy great distances through Earth. Sound waves can travel through air, but not through a vacuum. Light waves, however, are electromagnetic and can travel through a vacuum. That's why one can see explosions in space, but not hear them.

Science and Engineering Practices: Developing and Using Models

Allow students to play with waves in strings, ribbons, rubber bands, or toy spring coils. Have students draw pictures that show what they observed. Older students can add details, such as the relative amount of energy the waves carry and what kind of energy the wave might carry.

Wave Power

A door slams outside. The sound goes right to your ears. It's so loud! Those waves of sound must be really intense and tall!

A pin drops in your mother's bedroom, yet the sound doesn't make it to your ears. It barely makes a sound. These sound waves must be really short!

A car's headlight almost blinds you, but you could watch a candle flame for hours. What is the difference in these two light waves?

Draw this last pair of waves. Draw the waves of the bright light. Next, draw the waves of the candle. Explain each drawing.

....

Riding the Waves

It's a beautiful day. Wow! That's a tall ocean wave you're riding. Wave at the video camera. The camera will capture your image using light waves. Its recorder will capture the sound waves. We will be able to hear the wave crash—and maybe your laughter. And it will all be caught on camera. All of these waves transfer energy from one place to another. Continue this funny story using different kinds of waves. What happens next? Here are some other wave words you can include: seismic waves (from earthquakes), X-rays, microwaves, radio waves. Use at least three. Be sure to bring the story to a conclusion.

....

It's Invisible

Science
Notebook

Colored pencils

*The Future
Is Now!*

Science
Notebook

NGSS

1-PS4.B:
Electromagnetic
Radiation

4-PS3.B:
Conservation
of Energy and
Energy Transfer

4-PS4.B:
Electromagnetic
Radiation

CCSS

W.K.2, W.1.2,
W.2.2: Support
with Facts

W.3.3, W.4.3,
W.5.3: Imagined
Event

ADDITIONAL RESOURCES

PBS explores light and color at
http://pbskids.org/dragonflytv/
show/lightandcolor.html

Light by Daniel Nunn. Heinemann-
Raintree: 2012. (PreK–1)

Vampires and Light by Jodie Jensen
Shaffer. Capstone: 2013. (3–4)

LANGUAGE LINK		LEARNING SETTING
Explore:	Informative Writing	Individual
Dig Deeper:	Narrative Writing	Individual

Light

Science Information

Light (or radiant) energy transfers energy as waves or particles,
but at these grade levels light is most often described as waves (or
rays). These waves of energy travel in straight lines. We see objects
because light waves reflect from surfaces of objects and enter our
eyes. The surface texture of the object and material it is made of are
factors in how the waves reflect and what our eyes perceive. Mirrors
and shiny surfaces reflect all of the light at the same angle, so we see
a distinct image. Textured surfaces reflect light at different angles.
Whether a material is transparent, translucent, or opaque also
affects what we see. The transparent glass of a windowpane reflects
no light and allows it all to pass through. Then you see the object
reflecting light on the other side. Translucent materials scatter or
block some light. Opaque objects do not let light pass through at all
and cast a solid shadow behind it.

Science and Engineering Practices: Asking Questions and Defining Problems

Allow groups of students to discuss what they have learned about
light. You might use prompts, such as:

- What I've thought about windows helps to explain how light….
- I didn't know that reflected light….
- Shadows help to explain light because….

After discussion, challenge each group to define a problem they
might solve using light.

EXPLORE
It's Invisible

We can see flames in a fire. We can see smoke from the fire. But we can't see heat. We can feel its warmth.

Light comes from the sun. Its rays travel in straight lines. We cannot see them. But what if we could? Look how fast they travel! Draw an outdoor scene. Now place the sun in the sky. Draw lines from the sun to each object. Name two problems visible sun rays could cause.

Ready? Take

DIG DEEPER
The Future Is Now!

Can you imagine cutting through steel with just a beam of light? Seem impossible? Think lasers! Light from a laser goes in one direction only. It is a very intense beam of light, and a laser has only one color, or wavelength. That's why lasers have many specific uses. Stores use them to read bar codes. Doctors use them in delicate surgery. Think of two everyday tasks. How could they be made simpler with the use of a laser? Tired of mowing the lawn? Just swipe a laser across the lawn. Want to go for a swim in a hot swimming pool during the winter? Just focus the beam on the water and get ready to dive. Get the picture? How about two pictures? Provide illustrations showing two tasks you would accomplish using a laser's powerful energy. Explain each task and the role the laser plays. The future is now!

Ready? Take

PROMPT SUPPLIES

Clear Thinking ⋮ *Big Bend River*

Science
Notebook ⋮ Science
Notebook

Colored pencils

Drawing paper

Transparent
sheets
(commercial or
plastic sandwich
bags cut apart)

Tape

NGSS ⋮ CCSS

1-PS4.B: ⋮ L.K.5.C, L.1.5.C,
Electromagnetic ⋮ L.2.5.A: Real-Life
Radiation ⋮ Connections

4-PS3.A: ⋮ W.3.1, W.4.1,
Definitions ⋮ W.5.1: Support
of Energy ⋮ with Reasons

ADDITIONAL RESOURCES

This National Geographic video
captures "Fish With Transparent
Head Filmed" at http://video.
nationalgeographic.com/video/
news/transparent-fish-video-vin

Examine "Translucent Creature
Photos" at http://photography.
nationalgeographic.com/
photography/photos/
translucent-creatures/

Transparent and Opaque by
Angela Royston. Heinemann-
Raintree. 2008. (1–3)

LANGUAGE LINK		LEARNING SETTING
Explore:	Vocabulary	Individual
Dig Deeper:	Opinion	Individual

Transparent, Translucent, and Opaque

Science Information

Objects can be transparent, translucent, or opaque, which are properties that impact how light energy interacts with them. Translucent and transparent materials allow objects to transmit light—just not in the same way. Transparent materials, such as clean air; clean water; and clean, clear glass allow light energy to pass right through them without scattering. You can see objects clearly through them as if they are not there. Frosted glass, ice, waxed paper, and some plastics scatter light that passes through them. Objects on the far side of translucent materials appear blurry, but you may be able to determine what they are because of their darker shapes. Opaque objects simply stop the transmission of light. When they are in front of a source of illumination, they appear as dark shapes.

Science and Engineering Practices: Obtaining, Evaluating, and Communicating Information

Have students fold a sheet of paper into thirds. At the top of each section, students should add the labels "transparent," "translucent," and "opaque." Below each label, students should add the definition or draw a picture that shows the meaning. Then send students on a scavenger hunt, at home or at school, for examples of each kind of object.

Clear Thinking

Look closely at this picture of a stream. Notice the sunlight on the water. Water is transparent. Light energy passes through the water. When you're at the beach, you can see through the water to the sand. Stand closer to the stream of water. What can you see? Draw a picture of the water. Don't color it in! The water is transparent. Instead, draw objects in the water and show the bottom. Maybe there is a fish swimming by. Cover with the clear plastic. In your Science Notebook, list other examples of transparent objects.

Ready? Take 5!

Big Bend River

The nature club took a field trip to a local river. Here, large boulders cut through the water's surface, creating small rapids. The water was so transparent, light energy could pass right through it to reveal the river's sandy bottom.

"How's the fishing here?" one of the students asked the guide.

"Not so good," the guide replied. He then took them to a nearby pond. Here the water was translucent. According to the guide, the algae and tiny plants in the water allow little light to pass through. "And that's the secret for a good fishing spot. Fish feed on insects that feed on the algae."

But what about an opaque body of water? What does this water look like? What might cause it to look like that? What might the fishing be like in these waters? Why?

Ready? Take

Color

Science Information

What is one way we know that white light is composed of all colors? Rainbows! Light passes into and out of a drop of water, which acts like a prism. Each color in the spectrum bends at a slightly different angle based on its wavelength. Thus, we see the colors in a particular order every time.

Colorful objects appear in white light because certain wavelengths are absorbed and others reflected. A green object reflects green light, but absorbs the rest. Although students will recognize black and shades of gray as colors, scientifically, black is the absence of color, or a situation in which all wavelengths of light are absorbed. If that same green object is illuminated by red light, it appears black because the red light is absorbed, and there is no green light to be reflected.

Science and Engineering Practices: Obtaining, Evaluating, and Communicating Information

Have students draw scientifically accurate "you are there" pictures of rainbows. Students should show themselves with their backs to the sun and the rainbow in front of them. Have them label the white light of the sun, water droplets, and colors of the rainbow.

PROMPT SUPPLIES

Colors of the Rainbow	*The Colors of Summer*
Black paper	Science Notebook
Pastel markers	

NGSS	CCSS
1-PS4.B: Electromagnetic Radiation	W.K.2, W.1.2, W.2.2: Support with Facts
4-PS4.B: Electromagnetic Radiation	W.3.1, W.4.1, W.5.1: Claim with Evidence

ADDITIONAL RESOURCES

How can colors help scientists in their discoveries? One way is revealed at http://www.sciencechannel.com Search: "Atoms Signature Light"

"What is color?" Colm Kelleher has the answer at http://ed.ted.com/lessons/how-do-we-see-color-colm-kelleher

Colors of Insects by Laura Purdie Salas. Capstone: 2011. (K–2)

Superman Colors by Benjamin Bird. Capstone: 2014. (PreK–1)

EXPLORE
Colors of the Rainbow

Who is Roy G. Biv? Look around. He is in the room with you. Do you see red? What about orange or yellow? Can you see green or blue? How about indigo, a type of purple, or violet? Then you have just met Roy G. Biv. Each letter in this name is the sequence of colors in a rainbow. Sunlight holds all these colors together. We can't see them in the air. But raindrops or glass can break them apart. Draw a large raindrop on black paper in white or silver. Next, shoot a ray of white light toward the raindrop. Aim it at the left side of the raindrop. The white light has been blasted into the colors of the rainbow. Draw a rainbow coming from the right side of the raindrop. Below the drawing, answer this question: "Why did the light change from white to a band of many colors?"

Ready? Take

DIG DEEPER
The Colors of Summer

There is a debate going on. It is a debate about the colors we wear. In science, we know that dark colors absorb heat. That is why many people feel we should wear light-colored clothes in the summer. Why? Light colors reflect light, so the light can't turn into heat. Darker colors (especially black) absorb light, which changes into heat and makes us even hotter. Now, a different idea says just the opposite. This idea says dark colors are better in the summer because these colors absorb heat from our bodies, so dark colors keep us cooler. Which explanation do you think is right? Should we wear light or dark colors to stay cool in the summer? A white shirt or a deep blue one on the beach? Make a claim and provide evidence from science and your own experiences.

Ready? Take

Sound

Science Information

Consider this classic classroom demonstration for sound: Tightly tie a length of string to a doorknob or other stationary object and pull the string very taut. Pluck the tight string with your free hand. What happens visually explains the concept of sound as energy and how it moves. Plucking transfers energy to the string, which causes the string to move quickly back and forth, or vibrate. The vibrations carry the energy, or sound waves, and they travel outward through the medium of air to be detected by listening ears. Sounds are heard by our ears because the vibrating waves (energy) enter our ears and cause our eardrums to vibrate. The key to "hearing" is that sound energy requires a medium through which to travel (unlike light). Sound energy travels through solids, liquids, and gases, but not through vacuums, or the emptiness of space.

Science and Engineering Practices: Developing and Using Models

Students might examine how objects can be made to vibrate and the sound waves that are produced. They could then take turns presenting their sound and how it was generated. Additionally, they could show in a flowchart the path of energy that produced the sound.

PROMPT SUPPLIES

What's That Sound?	*Sounds Like*
Science Notebook	Science Notebook

NGSS	CCSS
2-PS4.A: Wave Properties	W.K.3, W.1.3, W.2.3: Imagined Event
4-PS3.A: Definitions of Energy	W.3.2, W.4.2, W.5.2: Support with Examples
4-PS3.B: Conservation of Energy and Energy Transfer	

ADDITIONAL RESOURCES

Sid the Science Kid explores sound waves at http://www.watchknowlearn.org Search: "Catch a sound wave"

The Physics Newton Channel will take you to Punk Science and "The science of sound and the power of rock." Look for it on the Internet.

Exploring Sound, a 4-book set, by Richard Spilsbury and Louise Spilsbury. Heinemann-Raintree: 2014. (2–4)

Making Sounds by Charlotte Guillain. Heinemann-Raintree: 2009. (PreK–1)

What's That Sound?

It's so dark outside tonight. I'm glad we are safe inside.

Shh! What's that sound? It's just a squirrel in the tree. It's dropping nuts onto a roof. The nuts cause the roof to vibrate.

Shh! What's that sound? It's just a knock on the front door. The knock causes the door to vibrate.

Shh! What's that sound? It's just a crack of thunder. The thunder causes the air to vibrate.

Make a list of the next three sounds you hear tonight. Beside each, tell what is vibrating.

....

Ready? Take

Sounds Like

Like heat and light, sound is another form of energy. Sound is the movement of tiny particles, or vibrations. These vibrations create sound waves, like the rattle of a drum or the boom of thunder.

A famous music conductor once said:

"We listen too much to the telephone and we listen too little to nature. The wind is one of my sounds. A lonely sound, perhaps, but soothing. Everybody should have his personal sounds to listen for—sounds that will make him exhilarated and alive, or quiet and calm. . ."

—Andre Kostelanetz

What about your personal sounds? Make a list of four different emotions. Connect a sound to each emotion. Next, identify a possible source for the vibrations that result in the sound.

©2016 Kaye Hagler and Judy Elgin Jensen from *Take 5! for Science*. This page may be reproduced for classroom use only.

World Map

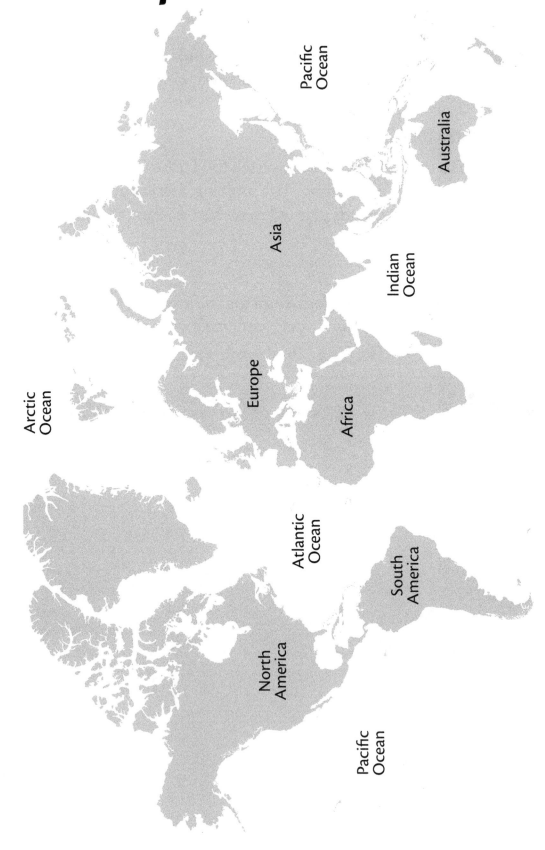

"Who Has Seen the Wind?"

By Christina Rossetti

Who has seen the wind?

Neither I nor you:

But when the leaves hang trembling,

The wind is passing through.

Who has seen the wind?

Neither you nor I:

But when the trees bow down their heads,

The wind is passing by.

Alphabetical Index

Bibliography

Coffey, J., Douglas, R., Stearns, C. (Eds). (2008). *Assessing Science Learning: Perspectives from Research and Practice.* Arlington, VA: NSTA Press.

Douglas, R, Klentschy, M.P. & Worth, K. (Eds.). (2006). *Linking Science & Literacy in the K–8 Classroom.* Arlington, VA: NSTA Press.

Fazio, X. & Gallagher, T.L. (2009). Supporting students' writing in elementary science: Tools to facilitate revision of inquiry-based compositions. *Electronic Journal of Literacy through Science, 8*(1). 1–15. Available: http://ejlts.ucdavis.edu. Retrieved March 2015.

Grant, M.C. & Fisher, D. (2010). *Reading and Writing in Science.* Thousand Oaks, CA: Corwin Press.

Hapgood, S. & Pallincsar, A.S. (2007). Where literacy and science intersect. *Education Leadership, 64*(4), 56–60.

Honig, S. (2010). What do children learn in science? A study of the genre set in a primary science classroom. *Written Communication.* 27: 87–119.

Jang, J.Y. (2011). The effect of using a structured reading framework on middle school students' conceptual understanding within the science writing heuristic approach. PhD (Doctor of Philosophy) thesis, University of Iowa. Available: http://ir.uiowa.edu/etd/1232. Retrieved March 2015.

Klentschy, M.P. (2008). *Using Science Notebooks in Elementary Classrooms.* Arlington, VA: NSTA Press.

McComas, W.F. (1998). The Principal Elements of the Nature of Science: Dispelling the Myths of Science. In W. F. McComas (Ed.) *Nature of science in science education: rationales and strategies* (pp. 53–70). Kluwer (Springer) Academic Publishers.

National Governors Association Center for Best Practices & Council of Chief State School Officers. (2010). *Common Core State Standards.* Retrieved from http://www.corestandards.org/

NGSS Lead States. (2013). Next Generation Science Standards: For States, By States. Available: http://www.nextgenscience.org/. Retrieved March 2015.

Osborne, J. (2002). Science without literacy: A ship without a sail? *Cambridge Journal of Education, 32*(2), 203–218.

Poe, M., Lerner, N. & Craig, J. (2010). *Learning to Communicate in Science and Engineering: Case Studies from MIT.* Cambridge, Mass: MIT Press.

Sampson, V., Enderle, P., Grooms, J., and Witte, S. (2013). *Writing to Learn by Learning to Write During the School Science Laboratory: Helping Middle and High School Students Develop Argumentative Writing Skills as They Learn Core Ideas.* Sci. Ed., 97: 643–670. doi: 10.1002/sce.21069

Thier, M. (2002). *The New Science Literacy: Using Language Skills To Help Students Learn Science.* Portsmouth, NH: Heinemann.

Thurston, A., Grant, G. & Topping, K.J. (2006). Constructing understanding in primary science: An exploration of process and outcomes in the topic areas of light and the Earth in space. *Electronic Journal of Research in Educational Psychology, 4*(1), 1–34.

Troia, G.A., Shankland, R.K. & Heintz, A. (Eds). (2010). *Putting Writing Research into Practice: Applications for Teacher Professional Development.* New York: Guilford Press.

Master List of Capstone & Heinemann-Raintree Books

Booklist from Chapter 2: Earth Science Prompts

Anatomy of an Earthquake by Renée C. Rebman. Capstone: 2011. (5–9)

Anatomy of a Tornado by Terri Dougherty. Capstone: 2011. (5–9)

Arctic Attack (from the Batman series) by Robert Greenberger. Heinemann-Raintree: 2010. (2–3)

A Refreshing Look at Renewable Energy with Max Axiom, Super Scientist by Katherine Krohn. Capstone: 2010. (3–4)

Changing Seasons Acorn set by Rebecca Rissman and Sian Smith. Heinemann-Raintree: 2012. (Pre K–1)

Comparing Bodies of Water by Rebecca Rissman. Heinemann-Raintree: 2010. (PreK–1)

Deep Oceans by Ellen Labrecque. Heinemann-Raintree: 2014. (1–3)

Earth (Astronaut Travel Guides) by Nick Hunter. Heinemann-Raintree: 2012. (3–6)

Earthquakes! by Renee Gray-Wilburn. Capstone: 2012. (1–2)

Engineering an Awesome Recycling Center with Max Axiom, Super Scientist by Nikole Brooks Bethea. Capstone: 2013. (3–6)

Exploring the Seasons, a four-set series, by Terri DeGezelle. Capstone: 2012. (K–2)

Fossil Fuels by Wendy Meshbesher, Eve Hartman. Heinemann-Raintree: 2010. (4–5)

Glaciers by Mari Schuh. Capstone, 2010. (K–1)

Hide and Seek Moon: The Moon Phases by Robin Koontz. Capstone: 2011. (1–3)

How Does a Cloud Become a Thunderstorm? by Mike Graf. Heinemann-Raintree: 2010. (3–5)

Hurricanes by Martha E.H. Rustad. Capstone: 2014. (PreK–2)

Inside the Water Cycle by William B. Rice. Capstone: 2010. (4–8)

Investigating Rocks: The Rock Cycle by Will Hurd. Heinemann-Raintree: 2009. (3–6)

Kit and Mateo Journey into the Clouds: Learning about Clouds by Cari Meister. Capstone: 2014. (K–2)

Landforms by Lynn Van Gorp. Capstone: 2009. (5–6)

Learning About Rocks by Mari Schuh. Capstone: 2012. (K–1)

Living Beside the Ocean by Ellen Labrecque. Heinemann-Raintree: 2015. (1–3)

One Giant Leap by Robert Burleigh. Philomel Books: 2009. (1–3)

Recycling: Reducing Waste by Buffy Silverman. Capstone: 2008. (3–6)

Saving Water: The Water Cycle by Buffy Silverman. Capstone: 2009. (1–3)

Shadows on My Wall by Timothy Young. Schiffer: 2012. (PreK–1)

Stars by Kristine Carlson Asselin. Capstone: 2011. (3–6)

Stars and Constellations by Nick Hunter. Heinemann-Raintree: 2013. (1–3)

Stars and Galaxies by Isabel Thomas. Heinemann-Raintree: 2012. (3–6)

Surviving Hurricanes by Elizabeth Raum. Heinemann-Raintree: 2012. (3–5)

Surviving Tornadoes by Elizabeth Raum. Heinemann-Raintree: 2012. (3–5)

The Big Picture: Climate, a 4-book set by Louise Spilsbury, Angela Royston, Catherine Chambers, and Sarah Levete. Capstone: 2011. (1–3)

The Milky Way by Martha E.H. Rustad. Capstone: 2012. (K–1)

The Planets of Our Solar System by Steve Kortenkamp. Capstone: 2011. (3–4)

The Power of Energy by Rebecca Weber. Capstone: 2011. (K–2)

The South Pole by Nancy Dickmann. Heinemann-Raintree: 2013. (1–3)

The Sun by Nick Hunter. Heinemann-Raintree: 2012. (3–6)

The Wettest Places on Earth by Martha E.H. Rustad. Capstone: 2010. (1–2)

The Whirlwind World of Hurricanes with Max Axiom, Super Scientist by Katherine Krohn. Capstone: 2011. (3–4)

The World's Most Amazing Rivers by Anita Ganeri. Heinemann-Raintree: 2009. (3–5)

Tornadoes: Be Aware and Prepare by Martha E.H. Rustad. Capstone: 2015. (PreK–2)

Volcano Explorers by Pam Rosenberg. Heinemann-Raintree: 2012. (1–2)

We All Have Shadows by Maryellen Gregoire. Capstone: 2014. (PreK–1)

What Is a Landform? by Rebecca Rissman. Heinemann-Raintree: 2009. (PreK–1)

When Volcanoes Erupt by Nel Yomtov. Capstone: 2012. (3–4)

Where Does the Sun Go At Night? An Earth Science Mystery by Amy S. Hansen. Capstone: 2011. (1–2)

Wind by Helen Cox Cannons. Heinemann-Raintree: 2015. (K–1)

Booklist from Chapter 3: Life Science Prompts

All About Animals, a four-book set, by Tammy Gagne. Capstone: 2015. (1–2)

Amazing Animal Adaptations, a four-book set, by Lisa J. Amstutz, Julie Murphy. Capstone: 2011. (1–2)

Amazing Animal Senses by John Townsend. Heinemann-Raintree: 2012. (1–3)

Animal Hibernation by Jeanie Mebane. Capstone: 2012. (1–3)

Animal Migration by Jeanie Mebane. Capstone: 2012. (1–2)

Animals that Live in Groups by Kelsi Turner Tjernagel. Capstone: 2012. (1–2)

Bonobos by Buffy Silverman. Heinemann-Raintree: 2012. (3–6)

Classifying Invertebrates by Francine Galko. Heinemann-Raintree: 2009. (3–5)

DNA and Heredity by Casey Rand. Heinemann-Raintree: 2010. (4–6)

Earth's Growing Population by Catherine Chambers. Heinemann-Raintree: 2009. (3–5)

Exploring Ecosystems with Max Axiom, Super Scientist by Agnieszka Biskup. Capstone: 2007. (3–6)

Food Chains and Webs, a six-book set, by Angela Royston: Capstone: 2015. (1–3)

Fossils by Richard Spilsbury and Louise Spilsbury. Heinemann-Raintree: 2011. (3–6)

Habitat Survival, a series of 8 books exploring different habitats, by Buffy Silverman, Claire Llewellyn, Melanie Waldron. Heinemann-Raintree: 2012. (2–4)

Invertebrates by Angela Royston. Heinemann-Raintree: 2015. (1–3)

Learn About Animal Behavior, set, by Kelli L. Hicks, Jeanie Mebane, Kelsi Turner Tjernagel. Capstone: 2012. (1–2)

Leaves by Melanie Waldron. Heinemann-Raintree: 2014. (2–4)

Ocean Food Chains by Angela Royston. Heinemann-Raintree: 2014. (1–3)

Plants by Melanie Waldron. Heinemann-Raintree: 2014. (4–6)

Producing Vegetables by Casey Rand. Heinemann-Raintree: 2012. (4–6)

Seeds Go, Seeds Grow by Mark Weakland. Capstone: 2011. (1–2)

Seeds (Plants) by Patricia Whitehouse. Heinemann-Raintree: 2009. (K–2)

The World of Food Chains with Max Axion, Super Scientist by Liam O'Donnell. Capstone: 2007. (3–4)

Understanding Animal Graphs (Real World Math-Level 3) by Dawn McMillan. Capstone: 2010. (2–3)

Understanding Photosynthesis with Max Axiom, Super Scientist by Liam O'Donnell. Capstone: 2007. (3–4)

Using Your Senses by Rebecca Rissman. Heinemann-Raintree: 2011. (PreK–1)

Booklist from Chapter 4: Physical Science Prompts

A Crash Course in Forces and Motion with Max Axiom, Super Scientist by Emily Sohn. Capstone: 2007. (3–4)

Adventures in Sound with Max Axiom, Super Scientist by Emily Sohn. Capstone: 2007. (3–4)

Aliens and Energy by Agnieszka Biskup. Capstone: 2011. (3–4)

All About Matter by Mari Schuh. Capstone: 2012. (PreK–2)

All About Temperature by Alison Auch. Capstone: 2011. (PreK–1)

Colors of Insects by Laura Purdie Salas. Capstone: 2011. (K–2)

Conductors and Insulators by Chris Oxlade. Capstone: 2012. (2–4)

DO-4U the Robot Experiences Forces and Motion by Mark Weakland. Capstone: 2012. (2–3)

Electricity by Louise Spilsbury and Richard Spilsbury. Heinemann-Raintree: 2013. (4–6)

Electricity All Around by Barbara Alpert. Capstone: 2011. (K–1)

Experiments with Sound by Isabel Thomas. Heinemann-Raintree: 2015. (2–4)

Exploring Sound, a 4-book set, by Richard Spilsbury and Louise Spilsbury. Heinemann-Raintree: 2014. (2–4)

From Crashing Waves to Music Download: An Energy Journey Through the World of Sound by Andrew Solway. Heinemann-Raintree: 2015. (3–6)

From Crude Oil to Fast Food Snacks: An Energy Journey Through the World of Heat by Ian Graham. Heinemann-Raintree: 2015. (3–6)

Ghosts and Aliens by Jodi Wheeler-Toppen. Capstone: 2011. (3–4)

How Do You Measure Weight? by Thomas K. and Heather Adamson. Capstone: 2011. (K–2)

Joe-Joe the Wizard Brews Up Solids, Liquids, and Gases by Eric Braun. Capstone: 2012. (2–3)

Light by Daniel Nunn. Heinemann-Raintree: 2012. (PreK–1)

Light and Sound by Wendy Meshbesher and Eve Hartman. Heinemann-Raintree: 2010. (4)

Magnets Push, Magnets Pull by Mark Weakland. Capstone: 2011. (K–2)

Making Sounds by Charlotte Guillain. Heinemann-Raintree: 2009. (PreK–1)

Making Things Move by Siam Smith. Heinemann-Raintree: 2009. (PreK–1)

Mass and Weight (Measure It!) by Barbara A. Somervill. Heinemann–Raintree: 2010. (3–6)

Mixtures and Solutions by Carol Ballard. Heinemann-Raintree: 2009. (4–5)

Positive Reaction! A Crash Course in Science by Sara L. Latta. Capstone: 2014. (4–5)

Sound and Hearing by Catherine Vietch. Heinemann-Raintree: 2009. (PreK–1)

Speed and Acceleration by Barbara A. Somervill. Heinemann-Raintree: 2010. (3–6)

Splat!: Wile E Coyote Experiments with States of Matter by Suzanne Slade. Capstone: 2014. (3–4)

Sports by Chris Oxlade. Capstone: 2012. (2–4)

Superman Colors by Benjamin Bird. Capstone: 2014. (PreK–1)

Temperature by Casey Rand. Capstone: 2011. (3–6)

The Attractive Story of Magnetism with Max Axiom, Super Scientist by Andrea Gianopoulos. Capstone: 2008. (3–4)

The Dynamic World of Chemical Reactions with Max Axiom by Agnieszka Biskup. Capstone: 2011. (3–4)

The Power of Energy by Rebecca Weber. Capstone: 2011. (PreK–1)

The Science of Speed, a four-book set, by Suzanne Slade, Lori Hile, Karen Latchana Kenney, Marcia Amidon Lusted. Capstone: 2014. (5–9)

The Solid Truth about States of Matter with Max Axiom, Super Scientist by Agnieszka Biskup: Capstone: 2009. (3–4)

Transparent and Opaque by Angela Royston. Heinemann-Raintree: 2008. (1–3)

Vampires and Light by Jodie Jensen Shaffer. Capstone: 2013. (3–4)

Zombies and Electricity by Mark Weakland. Capstone: 2013. (3–9)

Zombies and Force and Motion by Mark Weakland. Capstone: 2011. (3–4)

Maupin House *by*

capstone®
professional

At Maupin House by Capstone Professional, we continue to look for professional development resources that support grades K–8 classroom teachers in areas, such as these:

Literacy
Content-Area Literacy
Assessment
Technology
Standards-Based Instruction
Classroom Management

Language Arts
Research-Based Practices
Inquiry
Differentiation
School Safety
School Community

If you have an idea for a professional development resource, visit our Become an Author website at:
http://maupinhouse.com/index.php/become-an-author

There are two ways to submit questions and proposals.

1. You may send them electronically to:
http://maupinhouse.com/index.php/become-an-author
2. You may send them via postal mail. Please be sure to include a self-addressed stamped envelope for us to return materials.

Maupin House Publishing, Inc. by Capstone Professional
1710 Roe Crest Drive
North Mankato, MN 56003
www.maupinhouse.com
888-262-6135
info@maupinhouse.com